A Man's Guide
to Infidelity

CHEAT

Bill Burr,
Joe DeRosa,
*and*
Robert Kelly

**Simon & Schuster Paperbacks**

New York  London  Toronto  Sydney  New Delhi

Simon & Schuster
1230 Avenue of the Americas
New York, NY 10020

First Simon & Schuster trade paperback edition October 2012

SIMON & SCHUSTER and colophon are registered trademarks of Simon &
Schuster, Inc.

For information about special discounts for bulk purchases, please contact Simon
& Schuster Special Sales at 1-866-506-1949 or business@simonandschuster.com.

The Simon & Schuster Speakers Bureau can bring authors to your live event. For
more information or to book an event, contact the Simon & Schuster Speakers
Bureau at 1-866-248-3049 or visit our website at www.simonspeakers.com.

Designed by Ruth Lee-Mui

Manufactured in the United States of America

10 9 8 7 6 5 4 3 2 1

Library of Congress Cataloging-in-Publication Data

Burr, Bill.
    Cheat : a man's guide to infidelity / Bill Burr, Joe DeRosa, and Robert Kelly.
        p. cm.
1. Adultery—Humor.  2. Man-woman relationships—Humor.  I. DeRosa, Joe,
1977-  II. Kelly, Robert, 1970-  III. Title.
    PN6231.A28S27 1986
    818'.602—dc23
                                                            2012015139

ISBN 978-1-4516-4568-2
ISBN 978-1-4516-4569-9 (ebook)

*— To the wives and girlfriends —*

# CONTENTS

Every man wants a woman to appeal to his better side, his nobler instincts, and his higher nature— and another woman to help him forget them.

—*Helen Rowland,*
*author of* A Guide to Men *(1922)*

# INTRODUCTION

If you even glanced at the front cover of this book, you know what it's about. And if you're some weirdo who picks up a book and starts reading it without looking at the front cover first, this is a *book* for *men* about *cheating*. Let's get two things straight:

**1.** This book is gender specific for one reason: we're dudes. If we were chicks, we would've written a book to help women act like pigs. But we're not, so we didn't. Besides, women don't need any help in the deceit department. That's not a cheap shot. It's a respect thing. With this book, we're trying to up our game to reach their levels.

**2.** We're not telling you that you *should* cheat. We're telling you *how* to cheat. Understand that. If you do something you're not proud of after you read this book, don't start whining that "the book made me do it" or "it wasn't my fault."

You *did* want to do it, and it *is* your fault. And don't cry if you get caught. Getting busted is part of the game. Nothing is 100-percent guaranteed in life. The unexpected can always happen. So don't try to sue us after you get pinched, like some tub of shit who blames Taco Bell after a heart attack.

At some point, at some time, most men cheat. This book is predicated on that fact. We figured it was about time someone sat down and wrote a how-to on the subject. After all, if you're going to cheat, it's better for everyone if you don't get caught. This guide, if you take it seriously and pay attention, will teach you to cheat successfully.

Yes, seriously.

This book will take you step by step through the entire process of cheating, from choosing your mark to keeping glitter out of your pubes. We will break down this ancient art, present possible pitfalls, and provide you with solutions, all to make you a better cheater. This is information you need, especially in these harsh times when outrageous statements in divorce court such as "she's used to a certain lifestyle" or demands of forty grand a month in child support in order to feed a kid Froot Loops are not considered highway robbery. This is a very dangerous time to be a man if you are even *thinking* about stepping out.

The first rule of successful cheating is *Own your own shit.* If you're going to step out, you've gotta be a man about it. Control is key. Assess your situation, form a strategy, execute your plan, and take no prisoners.

Do you wanna get your dick wet or not? Then stop being a pussy.

A big part of not getting busted is recognizing what type of cheater you are or will be. This stems directly from your personality traits. There are guys who cheat for sex, guys who cheat for the rush, and guys who cheat for romance. Depending on your style, different rules and regulations apply to the approach. Not every cheat will play out in the same fashion. And women, diverse as they are, are also going to affect the circumstances. You need to be as familiar with her personality as you are with your own. We're going to cover all of this ground thoroughly.

See, guys tend to think that fucking around is black and white: you either do it or you don't. Looking at it that way is grounds for incrimination. The gray area is where to get all that sweet, discreet, extramarital ass. Infidelity is an incredibly complex endeavor, so you need to have your shit together.

When it comes to scoring some side puss, this book will be the best friend you've ever had. Of course, you could toss this book aside and go take advice from your real-life best friend. That's probably not a bad idea. After all, he's an actual person who loves you, and he might even buy you beers while you discuss the matter. It's just that he won't know what the fuck he's talking about.

We *do* know what the fuck we're talking about. Everything in this publication—facts, philosophies, opinions, advice—comes from legitimate, hands-on experience. We've cheated, and now that we have put that part of our lives behind us, we're sharing what we've learned. This information has been tried, tested, and lived. The "About the Authors" shit usually comes at the end of a book, but in this case, you should know why you can trust us.

## Bill Burr

I grew up in the suburbs of Boston. I got hammered, I got arrested, and along the way, I hung out with a lot of damaged people. I used to think it was because I found them interesting, but one day I realized that I was kind of fucked up too.

I did well in school through the eighth grade. But when I got to high school, I choked like Peyton Manning in the playoffs. So I began taking work in warehousing, sales, and construction. I hated having to be someplace. I hated having a boss. And I hated sitting across from someone as he reviewed my progress report, while I waited to see if I was going to make another twenty-five cents an hour.

To this day, I don't use GPS because I hate listening to that voice telling me what to do. "Make a left in two point two"—go fuck yourself, lady!

I know my anger at the GPS computer voice is misdirected. I tried working it out in therapy, but it never really took. Sitting around talking about your feelings and crying because somebody stole your crayons in the late 1970s was just stupid after a while. Shit happened. It sucked. And now I'm like this.

In 1992 I began doing stand-up. It was the perfect job for me. And during my seventeen years of nonstop touring, I've lived a life that I'm proud of. But there are a lot of things I've done that I'm not proud of. And *that's* the shit you are going to read about in this book.

My stories and insights into cheating are drawn from the most miserable and exciting periods in my life. Now I'm an old man—or at least too old to have kept living the way I was. I won't act as though I was a saint or judge you for what you're doing. No, I'm paying my knowledge forward.

Seriously: why should another man come home to find his wardrobe burned up on a three-foot patch of grass in front of his apartment complex when a retired piece of shit like me could offer some information that might prevent it? Finding the person you're supposed to be with isn't easy. You should be able to keep your sneakers. Good luck. This book will help.

## Joe DeRosa

I have been single for all of my thirty-four years on this planet, with the exception of a few short relationships. What the hell does a guy who's pretty much always been single know about cheating? I assure you: dating a woman is dating a woman, no matter how lax the circumstances appear to be. Being single teaches you a lot about monogamy. Some people—mostly the married, or "taken," folks—think that being single is a free-for-all; that you can do anything you want, whenever you want, with whomever you want. They picture your sexual life as being the kind of perverted indulgent adventure you could have only if you were touring with Def Leppard in the eighties.

This notion is about as true as saying, "Def Leppard are still as good as they were in the eighties." The idea that at any point in your life you can live like a wild gunman when it comes to sex and dating, free from any threat of consequence, is a pipe dream. Someone will eventually shoot you in the back.

*Just because you're single, it doesn't mean that you are not cheating.* We'll get into the logistics of that later in the book. But every woman you ever date, at every stage of the relationship, beginning with the very first time you sleep together, wants to know she's the one. (Of course, there are exceptions, but they are rare.) That brings up a very confusing question: If you can't sleep with other women when you're married, and you can't sleep with other women when you have a girlfriend, and you're not supposed to sleep with other women when you're just dating someone—when the hell *can* you sleep with other women? I'm here to answer that question. Throughout my years of bachelorhood, I've had to stay on my toes: cleaning up after myself, hiding, dodging phone calls, looking over my shoulder, changing names to protect the innocent. These devious behaviors aren't just for guys with wives and proper girlfriends. In fact, I've been at my worst when I've been most *un*committed.

My experience shows that having a few different women in your life is not just an ego stroke or an attempt to fuel your inner pimp, it's economical. Guys have biological clocks too. Once we hit our forties, if we're not married, in great shape, or rich, it's fucking *over*. No man wants to be the old drunk at the nightclub trying to pick up young chicks, or the creepy uncle at the family reunion freaking out his niece's girlfriends. "I'm still cool! I listen to Nirvana!"

I want to age with dignity. So sometimes I've juggled a bit in pursuit of "the one." It speeds things up and ensures that you're spending your time as effectively as possible. This approach forces you to shit or get off the pot—and start figuring out what you're really looking for.

## Robert Kelly

I am what you call a Rock Star cheater. Or what women call a piece of shit. I have cheated on every girl I've ever been with since the seventh grade except one: the first girl who cheated on me. That's right, I was cheated on first. I had hopes and dreams of becoming part of the utopian monogamist world that people have been telling me about my whole life. You know:

*Boy meets girl. Girl and boy kiss under an apple tree. Boy carves their names into the tree inside a heart. They stay together until they're old enough to get married. They have kids and pass down the same traditions over and over again till the end of time.*

It should be:

*Boy meets girl. Girl and boy kiss under an apple tree. Boy carves their names into the tree inside a heart. Then girl fucks boy's best friend in front of the rectory where boy's grandmother works caring for the priest from the local Catholic church. Girl gets pregnant with boy's best friend's child. Girl breaks up with boy. Then boy finds out his mom is cheating on his second stepfather with his soon-to-be third stepdad, who is Mom's boss. Boy cries in apple tree.*

That's real life.

Now, I'm not blaming that girl or anyone else for the road I took in life. Nor am I apologizing for it. I cheated for the past twenty years because it was fun and amazing. What a crazy fucking ride. To be with more than two chicks in one night! No, fuck that, to be with more than *four* chicks in one night!

Right now you're thinking, "Fuck that! No way you banged four different chicks in one night." Okay. I didn't have sex with all of them. I'm not superman. I'm a one-and-done kind of guy. But to have manipulated all those social situations just to get someone to be into me sexually was an amazing power to have. To be that close to getting caught and hurting someone you really don't want to hurt—but you just have to go for it. It's like Tom Cruise in *Top Gun*. He had to take it to the limit every time he got into that cockpit. He didn't want to hurt his wingman, but he had to feel the rush.

Looking back on all my relationships, thank God I did what I did. Otherwise I would have married—or even worse, had a family with—the wrong fucking girl. Not to mention, I never would have had all the fucking-great, holy-shit-wow sexual experiences I have had in my lifetime. I'll never have to look back wistfully and say I wish I'd been adventurous, because I did it all: from one-night stands; to girls who thought I would marry them; to the prostitutes and massage girls in this great country and all the way to the *termas* in Brazil and the women in the windows of Amsterdam; to all the other girls who touched my front bottom so I could feel that feeling of lust, passion, or dare I say love—even if it wasn't real. I could pretend for a moment. I could be whoever I wanted to be or whoever they wanted me to be.

I have been through it all: I have gotten caught, I have gotten away, and I have caught girls cheating on me. I have done every cheat in the book. And I completed my journey without losing everything, and found who I really was, who I really loved, and who really loved me. There were consequences, and some of them sucked. I had to question what really mattered. But that's what life is all about, isn't it?

This book gives you access to all of our wisdom. We've also talked to other cheaters, compared notes, and compiled the first known comprehensive document in this field to help other men. Of course, along the way we had to change a few names and details to protect the skanky.

This book will be good for you even if you're not cheating or would never think about cheating on the woman you love. Why? Because you're probably lying. If you are a man, the odds that you will commit some form of adultery are *92 percent.*

Yeah, we did just pull that number out of our asses, but you know we're right.

How does that old expression go? "If you're going to do something, you might as well do it right."

This book is not a pontification.

This is not a hypothesis.

This is not a theory.

This is HOW TO CHEAT.

# Chapter 1

# So You've Decided to Cheat

*Welcome to the Brotherhood*

Let us be the first to say, "Welcome."

Welcome to one of the largest fraternities known to man. The Fraternity of Cheaters is an organization that has been around since the beginning of time. It has no brochure, no sales call, no advertising whatsoever. So how do you join? It's easy. The invitation is in your balls.

Just about every man you know has a pair of balls. Even if one of your buddies has only one testicle, it doesn't matter. At some point, he too will become a member of the club: the sheer volume of sexual urges that every man fights through on a daily basis will guarantee it.

If females had any idea of the full extent of the uncontrollably filthy thoughts that run through our minds in the course of a single hour, they would be amazed that any man has learned how to tie his shoes, to say nothing of coming up with the iPod and Rogaine.

Yes, men are pretty impressive. We have invented trains, subways, automobiles, aeronautics, space exploration, cures for diseases, and more—all while trying to tune out the urge to go fuck something.

Members of the opposite sex may roll their eyes at what they consider to be a lame excuse. That makes sense: females aren't wired the way we are. Plus, men have been known to roll their eyes at women for talking about the difficulty of going through a pregnancy. So it all evens out.

This book is not about trashing women. It's about helping men deal with their sexual urges in a way that won't destroy all the good things that they've worked for. We are going to help you bang something on the side every once in a while without the whole thing blowing up in your face.

Now, let's get back to talking about your balls.

Your balls talk to you. And as a man, as much as you fight the urge, every now and then you have to listen.

Balls are why the brotherhood knows no boundaries. There are no secret handshakes, no monthly dues, and no halls of justice for meetings. Yet the fraternity thrives at the highest levels of power and influence and among the poorest of the poor. It is not held in check by the borders of any nation, the power of any church, or the iron hand of any dictator. Men do not listen to any of these organizations when it comes to their sexual decisions.

But they do listen to their balls.

Most of the men you pass walking down the street are your brothers in crime. And yes, many people consider cheating a crime. Our world defines man's most natural urge for sexual variety to be a personality defect. If he acts on that desire, he is a bad person, or a weak one, or simply a piece of shit.

The reason why no one talks about the brotherhood is simple: shame and guilt. Both of these emotions loom large in the game of cheating. This book exists to wipe them out.

For God's sake, you don't have to be a chemist (sorry, we're sick of the rocket-scientist reference) to notice the avalanche of powerful men taken down because they indulged in a little bit of strange. Men have lost everything that they've worked for because they got caught having sex. Think about that: seeing a beautiful woman and wanting to be with her is natural. But in this day and age, you have to be careful.

To most guys, sex means something only if they are in love with the woman they are having sex with. Other than that, it doesn't mean shit. But the rest of society begs to differ.

Enough with the fable that sex means something.

Golfers, football players, politicians, actors, real estate moguls, pilots—all these great men have accomplished legendary feats in the fields of sports, politics, business. You have read their names on the front pages of newspapers. They possess tremendous skill and intellect. But they have the cheat game of a high school freshman.

Playing a poor cheat game is no big deal if you're broke. What's your wife going to do? Take your Billy Bass?

However, if you're worth anything at all, it's time to tighten up your game. Divorce law is a bitch. Tiger Woods's ex-wife should be in the *Guinness Book of World Records* for becoming the first $350 million nanny in the history of the world. We don't care what her ex-husband did; no babysitter is worth nine figures.

We don't have the time, the brains, or the money to try to change the way the world thinks about cheating. But we can help men avoid the pitfalls that lead to being caught, being kicked out, and sleeping on an air mattress at forty-six years of age.

The authors of this book are all admitted members of the Fraternity of Cheaters. This is a good thing. Relationship experts on those Oprah-type shows always talk about men not being good at communicating. Well, we think it's time we got better at it. Thanks for the tip, ladies!

We will help you get what you want without damaging what you already have. Remember, you shouldn't have ice cream every day, but every once in a while it's a wonderful treat.

We'll show you the ropes, but first you must shed your shame and guilt. The easiest way to do this is to find somebody you identify with: a fellow swine who bears the same cross as you. There are plenty of unfaithful cocksmen throughout history who couldn't keep it in their pants. You're in great company. Trust us, if "not feeling bad about yourself" was good enough for these guys, it's good enough for you too.

# The Hall of Fame

## *Moses*

Here's a guy who freed an enslaved people and told a pharaoh to blow him, all while having two wives in his back pocket. Two! Two wives for the guy who brought us the Ten Commandments! You know, those tablets with the thing in them about not committing adultery because it's wrong? Sounds like old Mosey got to have his cake and eat it too. Now, you could argue that it wasn't infidelity, since he was married to both of them. Sure. And we could argue, "Go fuck yourself." Side slice is side slice, no matter how you slice it.

Now, let's avoid the blatant opportunity here for bad one-liners—"burning for bush," "parting the pink sea," "turning your staff into a snake"—and end on a tasteful note: when it came to fasting, Moses never included pussy. And neither should you.

## *Franklin Delano Roosevelt*

"A date which will live in infamy!"

FDR probably stole that line from his wife. We bet that Eleanor screamed it at him when she found out that he was banging her social secretary, Lucy Page Mercer. Can you believe that shit? We've all heard of a guy tagging his *own* lady helper, but not his wife's. Goddamn. That is what you call *talent*. And he managed to do it long *before* he became the thirty-second president of the United States—not that being leader of the free world (or having polio) ever stopped FDR from trotting around. He apparently used to have his mistress stay in the White House. On a typical day, he'd wake up, hold a staff meeting, write the New Deal, and then wheel into the guest room for a BJ while his wife was in the garden. Frankie D! He was a sly son of a bitch with some serious game. Most guys with two functioning legs can't manage to get laid. That limp-legged bastard was dustin' 'em off.

### Bob Marley

Potheads usually don't have a lot of motivation—but pussy can get even the most stoned of individuals up off the couch. Despite his heavy marijuana intake and the countless songs he wrote about how we all need to unify and care about one another, Bob found a way to justify popping off in plenty of "other women" who weren't his wife. *Plenty.* "One Love"? Not for this guy. After hearing about his self-serving and self-indulgent sexual infidelities, it's easy to understand how he pulled off sounding so sorrowful every single time he sang "Redemption Song."

### "Anonymous"

This next famous cheater is one of the all-time-great stand-up comedians. Considering that he's one of our own, he is going to remain nameless out of solidarity. For he is a true master of the craft whose comedy crosses all boundaries of race, religion, and social status. He is a hero to us all, and we respect the man too much to name him in this book. But let's just say that when he ate his Jell-O, he liked a little puddin' on the side.

### Arnold Schwarzenegger

This man is the American Dream. He moves to America from a country we couldn't find on a map, takes some 'roids, gets shredded, starts making movies, marries a Kennedy, and becomes governor of a state he can't even pronounce. Along the way, he puts himself out to stud within the confines of his own home by banging the housekeeper, has an illegitimate big-headed son, and is now trying to put the pieces back together.

But how can you pass judgment on Arnold? This guy accomplishes more in any given year than we three have accomplished in a lifetime—combined. His career stats are astounding: Mr. Universe at age twenty. Seven-time Mr. Olympia. More than a billion dollars in box-office receipts. Yet even this great man couldn't resist the temptation of convenience. Was she good-looking? No. Was she an intellectual? Probably not. Was she *present*? Yes. Game. Set. Match. Don't worry, Arnie, when you make *Terminator V,* the brotherhood will support you.

There have been a bunch of other well-known folks with the same poontang predilection that we have: Michael Jordan, Rudy Giuliani, Lyndon B. Johnson, John McCain, Ethan Hawke, Dwight D. Eisenhower, Hulk Hogan, David Letterman, Hugh Grant, and so on and so on and so on. Who the hell are you to say you're better than any of these guys?

That's right, you're not.

So the next time you're kicking yourself in the nuts because you told your wife you were "jammin' with the guys" so you could actually go hump your Bikram yoga instructor, stop and just remember:

All of our greatest inspirations would do exactly the same.

## Letting Go of Shame and Guilt

There is no way to get away with cheating unless you first deal with the feeling of guilt. Guilt causes you to run your mouth. Guilt puts a stupid look on your face the next time you see your girlfriend. Guilt causes you to confess.

Cheating and guilt are like eating hot wings and getting the shits. The two always seem to come packaged together, though you wish you could just enjoy the first by its lonesome. Well, as far as cheating is concerned, you can. Here's the good news: cheating is not your fault. (Shit, that's actually *great* news!)

And it's true, so let's say it again: *cheating is not your fault.*

Now, you say it. Go ahead. Say it out loud. Seriously. It's necessary for your growth.

Wow, did you actually just do that? If you didn't, congrats. You have dignity. If you did, you really might be a psycho. But at least you're committed.

Cheating has never been anybody's fault. Cheating is not merely a product of weak will, selfish indulgence, or a hard dick. There's some science involved here. Science is always your friend. Remember that. Whenever you need to combat society's self-righteous, imposing, and overly judgmental morality—what Jesus would do, protecting the environment, respecting other people, etc.—a strong scientific defense will usually give you a way out. It's hard to argue with facts. Still, many people will try.

Avoiding the truth is an endeavor as old as industry, and it has proven to be just as profitable. Avoiding the truth allows people to believe that there's a light at the end of the tunnel, that we're living to our fullest potential, and, most importantly, that we're justified in passing judgment on one another. That last one is a biggie. It's the reason that so many Americans consider cheating to be an epidemic and not a natural by-product of your libido.

Throughout history, many folks have embarked on sexual explorations with an Indiana Jones–like enthusiasm. Still, for the most part, our elders and forefathers have often attempted to hide their salacious appetites in the interest of making those who come after them feel like a gaggle of degenerate perverts. The bastards.

No other age group has mastered this wretched deception better than the "Greatest Generation." You wanna talk about legends? Holy shit. If Jesus's life already takes the title of "greatest story ever told," then the belt for "second greatest myth of all time" goes to the unjustly honored and needlessly praised Greatest Generation. These guys should have comic books and video games made about their trumped-up heroism and overexaggerated prowess.

One of the battles a cheater wages with himself is the nagging sense that not only is he a piece of shit, but also a new breed of piece of shit. This follows the line of thought that the overall moral code of today's man would be considered borderline illegal back in "the good ol' days." There are endless corollaries to this judgment about why we as a nation are fat, stupid, or addicted. And at the heart of it all are old guys like Clint Eastwood, calling the latest group of men the "pussy generation."

Evidently we are products of this awful age that we live

in. We got timeouts instead of beatings. We ate processed foods. We didn't go to church. And our marriages didn't work because of the sexual revolution.

Meanwhile, all of us drop to our knees and blow the past.

Nowhere is it more evident than in the term Tom Brokaw coined in his book of the same name: the Greatest Generation.

First of all, the number of people who reference the book yet have never read it is staggering. We haven't read it either, but being the pieces of shit that we are, we can spot an undeserved hand job from a mile away.

Second, the title is ridiculous. *The Greatest Generation*? You mean the generation that didn't let nonwhites play professional sports with white people? The generation that lived during a time when the date rapist was the victim, and the rape victim foreshadowed the "two-minutes-for-instigating" rule in the National Hockey League? That's the Greatest Generation?

We get it. They won World War II. They stopped the spread of the Nazis and the Rising Sun. Then they came home, got hammered, and beat their wives with a mop handle because they were angry that they'd accidentally drunk from the "colored only" water fountain. Obviously, we're not talking about each and every person from that generation, but there is a reason that Brokaw wrote that book, and not Ed Bradley.

That's the funny thing about that period in our history. It's either romanticized or ripped to shreds. Take baseball: old-timers either talk about how great it was to live in New York City and be in the eye of the rivalry among the Brooklyn

Dodgers, the New York Yankees, and the New York Giants, or they talk about what Satchel Paige could have done if he was allowed to play in the MLB during his prime and Jackie Robinson's struggles as the first black man to break the color barrier. But they never tell those stories at the same time.

Our point is, don't romanticize the past. There *were* a lot of great things going on: we made better cars, people read more, and a lot more products were manufactured within our borders. But as for the people, they were just like us. There were doctors, lawyers, serial killers, kidnappers, pedophiles, racists, sexists, war mongers. And don't forget the senator named Joe McCarthy, who, if he were alive today, would probably be hosting a nationally syndicated radio program and claiming that all Muslims and Hollywood types are evil and need to be purged from this country. And last but not least, there were also *pussyhounds*!

Not only pussyhounds, but legendary pussyhounds. Greatest Generation pussyhounds, with wives and kids. When you hear about President John F. Kennedy being a war hero, the story never goes, "He saved his crew, swam to safety . . . Oh, and he also fucked Marilyn Monroe on a replica Betsy Ross flag in the White House." Just think about JFK's level of cheating. He had the Secret Service watching him 24/7, so they *knew* what he was doing. And then they had to look the First Lady in the eye later that day. Sound familiar? This shit is timeless.

Yet the popular mind-set is that the only way to get laid back then was to either get a hooker or to marry the girl you were with so she'd finally give you some.

We thought that was the prevailing rule of society up

until the late 1960s: Woodstock, the Summer of Love, and all that. Then one day Bill was golfing and got paired up with a seventy-five-year-old World War II vet.

## Bill's Story

He asked me if I had a girlfriend, and I told him, "No, but I'm kind of seeing some girl I worked with." Without missing a beat, he said, "Oh yeah? Is she any good?"

My jaw dropped. I knew old people had to have fucked at some point in their lives, for the simple fact that my friends and I existed, but I never knew they were *into* it. I thought they had sex only to procreate and were all uptight about the subject.

When I expressed my shock, this old man said, "Every generation thinks they're the first ones who ever fucked."

He then went on to tell me that while being a married man, he used to fuck some redheaded girl with green eyes up against a tree during the day, and she loved it. He fathered four children with three different women, and the "other woman" had been his big weakness in life.

I was initially looking at this old man like he was some stellar example of what we as a country used to be, but after talking to him for about three holes, I was wondering why he wasn't on Maury Povich.

"You gotta fuck 'em from behind if you want 'em to cum . . ."

In life, you have what people *say* is happening and what's *really* happening. And what was *really* happening with the Greatest Generation was a whole lot of fucking. How do you think we ended up with the baby boom generation? Do you think that all of those kids were legitimate?

How many abortions do you think there were? How many sons of bitches were there? How many bastards? How many town whores? These words and phrases exist for a reason: because people have always fucked around.

When people get old, they lie about their lives. They add accomplishments and leave out the missteps. Don't listen to them. They are just like you and me. And anything you're doing, they already did. So drop your guilt! Nothing you are thinking about doing is new. You are no better or worse than the people who came before you. Someday you're going to be old, and you're going to be happy you tagged that chick up the street. But it's up to you. Either do it or don't. But for the love of God, stop feeling guilty about it. You're just like they are—but a lot less racist, hopefully.

People have been fucking around since the beginning of time. It's natural. If you see a beautiful woman, you want to fuck her. The problem is, sometimes you already have a beautiful woman in your life. So what do you do? You read the rest of this book, and then you fuck her too.

## We're Not Fuckin' Penguins

There's a reason your little peter starts to spring and stir every time you lock it in your shorts: you're a mammal. Mammals wanna bang. Always. And aside from human beings, no mammalian species on earth practices monogamy. Fine, the penguins do. But there's an exception to every rule. Also, it's cold as balls where they live. If you're lucky enough to find some tush to keep you warm in a horrific climate like Antarctica, hang on to it and don't look the gift horse in its mouth.

Some might say that we human beings are the most elevated souls on the planet and therefore should adhere to a higher code of ethics than the common forest dweller. Well, this stance is logical only if you dismiss the fact that we are, in fact, animals. We came from the forests, jungles, mountains, and canyons. You know, the places where all the animals live? Some people still live there too. We don't understand why, but they do. Most of us have figured out how to get into town houses or at least apartments by now.

The next logical argument is that, yes, we are animals, but an advanced strand of animal, with more civilized be-havior. This notion is also false. We murder, maim, spread disease, and scare the shit out of one another as much as any lion, tiger, or bear ever has. And if you think that getting a nut belongs next to any of the activities listed in that last sentence, you're either a moron, a sicko, or both.

Other than the penguins, we're the only ones doing this single-partner shit. And there's a bunch of other mammalian species on the planet. None of them believes in or prac-tices romantic love. None. Other animals don't even know what the fuck romance is. They're all using sex for the one and only reason that it truly exists: procreation. Dogs bone shamelessly in the park and create uncomfortable eye candy for all the Frisbee players. Deer stick it in each other end-lessly and multiply prolifically so they can then run across a country road and total your car. And rabbits? You know how *they* pork. Oh yeah, *pork*. Don't forget pigs. Or cats or gerbils or rats or anything else on the planet that's out there getting some. Granted, they don't have the option of masturbation.

All right, monkeys do. (These frigging exceptions to a rule really trip you up when you're on the roll to making a great point.)

So the monkeys can masturbate. We know this because they do it in public. You know what? So do we sometimes. Not *we* meaning "we, the authors of this book," but *we* as in "mankind." Not *human*kind, mind you: *man*kind. Women don't finger away in public. Only guys give it a crank on the subway or outside your kitchen window. How about that? We have yet another thing in common with our closest genetic companions, the apes.

No other animals have the luxury of self-pleasure. Maybe they can hump the occasional unsuspecting leg, but that's about it. You, though, can sit at home and chafe yourself to Pornotube.com if you're so inclined. But for most guys, pulling at themselves isn't enough. There's a greater, biological urge: your sole purpose for being on this planet is to plant your seed. It's what got us out of the forest in the first place. It's the motivation for everything. So why would you turn your back on the act that made us so abundant?

Don't be a dick. Your seed creates life, life leads to a family, a family needs support and protection, protection and support are provided through a job, a job makes you money, a better job will make you more money, more money will allow for a better life for your family, a better life makes your family happy, a happy family means a happy wife, a happy wife gives you ass, ass is what you plant your seed in, and so on, and so on, and so on.

See all the good things that come from sex? One day you're tagging some hairy chick next to the fire in a cave, and the next thing you know you're on Wall Street, popping a high-priced call girl in between stock swindles.

But if the point of everything is procreation, and procreation leads to babies, does that mean that cheating is kosher so long as you're making babies? *No! Don't make any babies, you asshole!* The means don't always justify the ends. That pussy thirst is always going to be there, regardless of what happens once you drop a load. Whether you release your protein into a loved one, a stranger, a condom, or the air, the thirst will have been quenched—at least for the time being.

What you need to do is to trick your psyche into believing you've been reproducing, which is easy. All it takes is an orgasm to do it.

## Fuck Monogamy

We're not really sure about how, why, or where it started, but the practice of monogamy dates to ancient Mesopotamia and Egypt. It's been going on for quite some time, although it didn't quite have the same restrictions back then as it does now. In some of these old cultures, being monogamous meant that you stayed with your woman so long as she could crank out a baby for you. If she couldn't do so within the first year, she was outta there. Nice, huh? Those Babylonians really knew how to make a gal feel special.

Despite monogamy's long history, modern-day commitment to the cause is weak. Statistics always help support an argument; people seem to be impressed when they see numbers. So we've pasted below the results of the Standard Cross-Cultural Sample on extramarital sex in fifty different cultures, which tells you how many men and women from different places around the world are fucking around.

| Extramarital Sex by Men | | Extramarital Sex by Women | |
|---|---|---|---|
| Universal | 6 cultures | Universal | 6 cultures |
| Moderate | 29 cultures | Moderate | 23 cultures |
| Occasional | 6 cultures | Occasional | 9 cultures |
| Uncommon | 10 cultures | Uncommon | 15 cultures |

Wow. The lack of dedication to the single-sex-partner practice is universal among men and women. Very few people really practice this shit these days.

But not every old-school culture was gung ho about monogamy, either. You know those creepy things called "swing parties" that take place in secret locations and are attended by weirdos and sex freaks? Well, those used to take place all the time back in the day, and nobody gave a shit.

As a matter of fact, they were celebrated. The ancient Romans and Greeks had orgies like nobody's business. These people were sucking and fucking and eating grapes within the pillars of every bathhouse in town. In Greece, sex was a religious ritual, for Christ's sake. Our churches didn't do cool stuff like that when we were growing up. All in all, the Greeks and Romans were having a lot of fun, celebrating sex, and banging away. But then, somewhere in the midst of Rome falling and Julius Caesar getting stabbed at the Theatre of Pompey, the good times stopped rolling.

But enough about Europe. Let's talk about what happened when the Puritans landed in New England and laid the foundation for Western civilization as we know it. The

Puritans. Shit. The fucking root word in their name is *Pure,* so how much fucking fun do you think these guys were up for when they got here? None. Exactly. No wonder we've got such a sex complex in the United States: a constant stream of porn being produced and sent out over the Internet; billboards with half-naked women on them; magazines full of tits and ass; movies that show everyone from Halle Berry to Anne Heche getting nailed; TV shows that parade sexpots around like floats at the Puerto Rican Day Parade; and hookers and whores who strut our streets. You'd think with all that stuff in our faces, we'd have a better understanding of what our basic yearnings are, but we don't. That's why, instead of having stupendous orgies like they did overseas, we have unsettling sex parties like they do in John Waters movies.

In America, people want to hide their sex, which is why cheating is held in such disrepute. It's become something shameful to be hidden and not discussed. If it weren't, it wouldn't be called *cheating.* It'd be called *cleaning,* because that's all it is: rinsing out the old pipes. Of course, that's not a blanket explanation for why every guy steps out, but it's as close as we can get. Cheating is usually a direct result of buildup. Look at it as dusting the vents. Doesn't sound so bad anymore, does it?

Aside from its social, religious, and other influences throughout history, infidelity's biggest motivator has probably been the concept of fairy-tale romance. Finding your soul mate, riding off into the sunset, time standing still when your eyes lock from across the room, standing on her lawn with your boom box a la John Cusack in the flick *Say Anything,* taking the stripper "away from all this" and to a better place, rolling around in a meadow—these things are bullshit. They don't happen. Ever. But from birth, we're told they do. Especially girls. By the time they take their first steps, they're building a dream house for Ken and Barbie or being read stories of princes rescuing princesses.

Most guys don't get the heavy-handed treatment, but this crap still creeps into our psyche via the endless stream of phony sentimental propaganda spewed out by Hollywood every year. Even if you hate romantic comedies and melodramatic love stories, there's no way to avoid them. They're everywhere. Constantly. Just turn on the TV for ten seconds, and you'll see some nonsensical, false interpretation of what love is supposedly like.

That stuff may seem harmless, but trust us, it's lethal. It creates an emotional expectation that can never be fulfilled. It also breeds personal expectations that are unfair to place on yourself. What happens is, you end up getting into relationships and, when it's not all fireworks and horseback rides, you feel that you're flawed somehow. Like you're missing some key component that everybody else has. But you're not missing anything. You're feeling exactly how you should be feeling. It's natural. And, by the way, everybody else feels like that too. But nobody wants to talk about it because every single person who feels like this thinks he's the only one.

So when you get these basic human urges to cheat, everything you've ever learned about love prods you to think it's contradictory to being a decent person. That's bullshit. And it's the media's fault. Well, your parents could have stepped in and taught you a thing or two about how shit really works.

In a perfect world, Mom and Dad would tell their kids, "It's okay not to get married. But if you want to, that's totally cool." They'd also explain, "If you stray from your wife's womanhood once in a while, it's no harm, no foul. Just don't be an asshole or reckless about it. And if you're perfectly happy committing to one vagina for your entire life, well then, that's great too." Movies and TV shows would do the same. There wouldn't be any more of this nonsense of possessed lovers bounding toward each other through a tranquil meadow and then falling into each other's arms. You'd just see regular people living regular lives and doing regular things.

Which may or may not include banging on the side. But either way, it'd be normal.

### "But What About the Sanctity of Marriage?"

For our purposes, marriage is basically the same thing as any other monogamous relationship. Even if you're not wearing a ring, the expectations are the same: you eat together, sleep together, socialize together, and, most importantly, you don't bang anybody else. Even if you don't live with your girlfriend, any serious relationship exists within roughly the same parameters of marriage. So stop kidding yourself. That being said, where did marriage even come from? We researched it but were unable to pinpoint an exact origin. All we found was that there are a bunch of legends about how it started. That's right, legends, as in "of Sleepy Hollow," or "of the Lone Ranger," or "of Motherfucking Zelda," for Christ's sake.

Legends are fantastic stories full of superhuman characters, swashbuckling adventure, and, most of all, tons of shit that isn't goddamn possible in real life. That's why they're fucking legends and not the boring-ass stories you had to read in your sixth-grade American history book.

A word like *legend* should never be associated so closely with the origins of an institution as rigid as marriage. We'd settle for *yarn, cock-and-bull story,* or even *tall tale,* but not *legend.* No way.

Once you dig back far enough into the past, you'll find that the average person didn't even understand the concept of time, much less have the ability to record it or its events properly. Jump forward a bit, and you'll find a bunch of folks who actually thought poems, myths, and fireside stories were legitimately informative.

Can you imagine? There were people who actually believed something like Homer's *Odyssey* was based in fact. That'd be like you thinking *Star Wars* wasn't a movie but documentary battle footage from actual space conflicts.

We know: we wish it were too, but it isn't. And, disappointed as we all may be, understanding the distinction between fiction and reality is a greater gift than a light saber could ever be.

Here's the point: the practice of marriage, despite predating even the most primitive of modern societies, is still the primary way we humans organize ourselves. Three-quarters of the world's population—at some point in their lives, whether it works out or not—get hitched.

Something doesn't add up here. Anybody else have any other archaic practices they'd like to uphold? Burning someone at the stake? Drowning a witch? Going to church?

It'd be different if the bonds of holy matrimony sufficiently and fairly reflected the times we're living in, but they don't. There used to be an age when marriage did that. Once upon a time, people didn't live to be ninety-seven, women weren't allowed to work or vote, men couldn't be openly gay, and narrow-minded people thought that the only way society could function properly was systematically.

All of those artificial restrictions were, are, and will always be horseshit. Anything that works better when individuals have fewer rights and die sooner needs to be reworked. But marriage isn't going anywhere.

Sure, the rules and ramifications of marriage have changed over time. But that just means that you're no longer able to buy your wife, tie the knot with a thirteen-year-old, or be considered incestuous if your partner coincidentally has the same last name that you do. Some Mormons can be wed to multiple partners. Well, the women can't, just the men. In some other cultures, women don't even get to keep their clitorises, yet those guys are running around with five different deposit slots. That doesn't seem fair. In most places, gay guys still can't get married, and they get beat up and discriminated against just for demanding the privilege.

This marriage shit shows us the flaw of man through the absurdity of his rules—a bunch of self-centered, egotistical, and sometimes hateful rules that severely need to be modified.

Marriage is supposed to be about love and compassion, but those two things fly out the window when dealing with the laws governing it. Horseshit rears its ugly head again.

And once horseshit shows up this many times, you have to realize that the institution you're dealing with is, at best, severely flawed and never, never at all sacred.

Love is sacred, not marriage. And love doesn't have a specific set of rules. The laws governing marriage don't have a goddamn thing to do with how invested or committed you are to your life mate.

Rules are usually annoying, stupid, and flawed by man. There's a certain effect that rules have on a person. Basically, they make you want to break them. Marriage is no exception. Just like when your second-grade teacher told you not to laugh in class, your parish priest told you not to talk in church, and your mother told you not to look in your dad's sock drawer when they weren't home, the inventors and overseers of marriage tell you not to fuck when the wife's not around.

Now look, we're not saying it's impossible to stay faithful to one person for the rest of your life. It's possible. But it's not unnatural if you can't. Monogamy is like an iPhone. It can be a wonderful thing, so long as you're willing to put up with the bugs. We love the iPhone. We think it's great. But if any of us saw a guy throwing his against the sidewalk, shattering it into pieces while yelling, "Fucking iPhone! I'm getting a Droid!" we'd understand.

Another thing about monogamy is that it's all too frequently tested in controlled environments. The experiment is safe and the outcome is predictable. It's easy to be a champion of faithfulness when you live in a small town, lead a quiet life, and, outside of your wife, essentially have nothing fuckable around you. Your libido is going unchallenged. But try taking a good-hearted "family man" out of solitary confinement and drop him into the general population in New York City, Los Angeles, San Francisco, Chicago, Philadelphia, Boston, or any other major city where tits and ass litter the streets like soda cans and cigarette butts. Let's see what a proponent of monogamy he is then. If he keeps it together, he's the real deal. If not, it's nobody's fault but the designer of his genetic makeup.

# TRUE CHEAT

**Account by Keith Robinson, comedian, actor**

**Outcome:** *fail*

I used to live in Philadelphia, and I would always drive up to New York with Big Jay Oakerson and Kevin Hart, two comedians. One time I was going alone to see this girl I was cheating with, but I told my chick that I was going with Jay and Kevin, because she wanted to go to New York really bad that day. She kept saying, "Damn, I just wanna go to New York!" And I'm like, "I can't take you to New York because me and my friends are in this basketball league. We're gonna play all day and then go out to eat and all that."

"Well, why are you so dressed up, then?" she asked.

Good point. I had on white silk pants, nice wingtip shoes. I was lookin' good. My cologne was just right. There was no indication of a basketball being within five hundred miles of me. But my dumb ass thought the easiest thing to do was to say that I was going to play basketball. So I was like, "Oh, um, that, well, yeah . . . you see, we do that up front. We . . . dress up."

So I leave. I'm driving along in my car, thinking I got away with it, when I look in the rearview mirror and see my girl right behind me in another car. And she can't even drive! I'm in a high-speed chase trying to shake her, and she's running right through lights, right after me.

I called Kevin, panicked. "Kev, come outside! Hurry up! And bring your basketball with you. She's following me, and I can't shake her!" I turn down Spring Garden Street, and she's right behind me. I turn, she turns. And I'm still on the phone, yelling, "Kev, get outside!! Get your clothes and get outside!"

So I pull up to Kev's door, brakes screeching. She's right behind me. I get out, and little dumb Kev comes out with shorts on, dribbling a basketball. I say to him, "What are you doing? You ready to go ball, right?"

When she got out of the car—I'm just looking at her like a jackass—she took a can of Pepsi that she had in the backseat, shook it up, and sprayed it all over my white silk pants. I had also just gotten my car detailed, and it was nice and shiny. So she took a can of motor oil and poured it all over the windows. It was awful.

I went home and changed into some bullshit clothes, and now my chick didn't even wanna go to New York anymore.

And that was that.

## The Fuckup

How many fuckups can one man possibly commit when attempting to cheat? Let's start at the beginning. Keith told his girl he was going to run rock while he was wearing wingtips and dress slacks. Holy shit. Talk about the portrait of a slacker in action.

This was the laziest thing we'd ever heard of anybody doing since—well, ever. When Keith's girl called him on his nonsense, the best excuse he came up with was, "We get dressed up before playing ball." Like he was playing for the fucking Boston Celtics and on his way to a playoff game. Keith might as well have told his chick that the press gathers at the street court and that he needed to be dressed up for the news photos. That fib would have been just as goddamn believable.

Next on Keith's list of gargantuan fumbles was bringing his buddies into his lie without telling them. So when Keith was Starsky and Hutching his way to Kevin Hart's house, he was in a goddamn panic, not only trying to get Kev to save his ass, but also trying to translate all the basic details of what was happening. An unexpected high-speed chase is tense enough. You shouldn't also have to worry about explaining logistics while you're doing eighty around a corner. And Keith was lucky that Kev was home. Actually, that didn't matter. Keith pulling up to an empty house wouldn't have made a bit of difference. Let's not forget that he ended up with Pepsi-soaked pants and oily windows.

Here's something else: because Kev had no idea what was going on, he came out of the house in traditional basketball gear—another strike against Keith's rock-solid "We gussy up before the game" explanation. At this point, it was painfully obvious that the only rim Keith was planning to shoot in was some other broad's asshole.

Lastly, Keith underestimated what his girl was capable of doing. He was dealing with a woman who couldn't drive but was willing to reenact a scene from *The Fast and the Furious*. That's some hard-core shit. We're actually shocked that Keith's woman didn't simply call his friends to double-check his story. Since Kev and Jay had no clue about what Keith was up to, their accidental confessions would have shut down his plans pretty fucking quick. Most women would avoid phoning a guy's pals because they'd be scared of coming off as too aggressive. But this woman clearly did not give a fuck. Also, she could have saved herself some gas, not to mention motor oil and Pepsi.

So, just to recap: Keith told the most unbelievable lie ever, didn't inform his buddies of his deception, made light of his girl's capabilities, and almost got himself killed in a car wreck. The only thing he did right was get soaked.

That made us laugh. A lot.

# Chapter 2

# You and Your Dick

## An Owner's Manual

If you compiled a list of every dangerous thing that could possibly hurt someone or end his life, it would go from here to China and back again. Topping the list would be the usual suspects: drugs, guns, war, poisonous snakes, serial killers, natural disasters, nuclear meltdowns, etc, etc. If you read that list of dangers, people would nod in agreement, like one of those moron families on *Family Feud* who clap in unison, shouting, "Good answer! Good answer!"

Along with all of these dangers, you could find reams of information that exist for the sole purpose of helping human beings to avoid hurting themselves. For instance, despite the fact that most people do not own a gun, most still know that you have to make sure the gun isn't loaded and that the safety is on before you clean it.

Think about how much safety information has been beaten into your head. How long are you supposed to wait to go swimming after you eat? What is the proper way to look for traffic before crossing the street? If you are about to stick a metal knife into a toaster to dislodge a Pop Tart, what do you have to do first?

The answers spill out of your mouth as if you were the Manchurian candidate.

But despite all the dangers examined and all the information out there to help you avoid said dangers, where on that list of potential pitfalls is *having a dick*?

We'll tell you where it is: *nowhere.* There is no information out there to help a man deal with the fact that he has a dick. You inherit its awful power and responsibility the day you're born, and it's up to you to figure out how to handle it.

That's crazy.

Having a dick is one of the most dangerous things on the planet. How many people are eaten by sharks each year? How many guys lose everything they've got because of their dick? Yet the Discovery Channel has Shark Week every other fucking month. Why doesn't it have Dick Week? That would be the scariest seven days in the history of television.

"He came from an impoverished background. Most of his childhood friends ended up dead or in jail. But despite the odds stacked against him, he persevered and built a one-man empire the likes of which have never been seen since the beginning of time. Then he stuck his dick in the wrong chick and lost everything." Get Danny Elfman to write the score, and you'd have a blockbuster hit.

Hanging between your legs is an organ that can have you sleeping on a futon in your midfifties because of one stupid decision. Your dick is like the tiger that attacked that magician dude during a show in Vegas. You think it's your buddy, and then one day it grabs you by the fucking throat, and things are never the same again. So where is the warning label?

When cocaine resurfaced in the 1970s, it was initially considered no more addictive than caffeine. By the time the eighties came around, there was a nationwide campaign to expose the drug called the "Big Lie." But the dick has yet to feel any sort of backlash from pop culture. It's never been seen on a magazine news program, stepping out of a limo and refusing to comment after it has ruined yet another guy's life.

You see these stories time and time again: "Rich, powerful man, brought down by the wrong piece of pussy." During the fallout, you get no real information, only judgment: "He's a piece of shit!"

Or maybe a couple of street jokes: "Brett Favre, Tiger Woods, and Bill Clinton walk into a bar . . ."

The one sliver of advice you get during the entire debacle is, "Hey, man, you gotta keep it in your pants."

That's it? That's all we get? Thousands of pages have been written on the rare mystery of spontaneous human combustion. But for the entire "I have a dick, what do I do?" question, all we get is "Keep it in your pants." That is basically the dick-advice equivalent to the "Just Say No" drug campaign of the 1980s. You're fighting the laws of nature. You are also fighting a puritanical philosophy that isn't natural, considering the amount of effort it takes to "keep it in your pants."

Okay, so a bunch of preachers or Bible thumpers would argue that a certain good book has tons of information about the dangers of lust and, basically, the predicament of having a dick. We've tried to readeth that booketh of metaphoreths, and we've learned that a lot of these same flimflammers, despite their years of study, still have a difficult time keeping it in their *own* pants.

Forget Jesus freaks. The most interesting twist to the dick debate is women. They know more about the dangers of a man and his dick than men do. When you think about women's ability to manipulate men, so much of their game plays off the fact that most men think with their dicks.

Women play both sides of the equation. When they want to make you feel bad, they'll act like you're a horny chimp and they are disgusted by your day-to-day behavior. Other times, they'll use the fact that you think with your dick to their advantage.

That's why most of them lead us around by our noses. Basically, they know how weak we are. They know how to put out that "Maybe I'll fuck you . . ." vibe in order to get out of us exactly what they want. So how is it that they know more about it than we do? Simple: because we're morons. It's one of the side effects of having a dick. It causes you to act before you think.

Acting before you think is page one in the unwritten pamphlet about the dangers of having a dick. That is the exact thing that gets most men into so much trouble. Their dick gives them an impulse, and they immediately spring into action, never realizing that no real plan of attack has been devised.

When was the last time your dick came up with a good plan? Oh, it's got some great ideas, but when was the last time it came up with a good plan beyond "Do it"?

That's your dick's entire plan: "*Do it.*"

Forget preparation, forget looking for possible pitfalls, forget everything. If your dick were a person, it would be on *America's Dumbest Criminals*.

*So why the fuck are you listening to it*?

Your dick is basically an idiot. Your dick is like your thirty-five-year-old unmarried friend who likes to wear Hawaiian shirts and still tries to hit on twenty-two-year-olds. It never matures, but you do. In most social situations, you know better, but the problem is, you've been listening to your dick for so long, you're afraid to strike out on your own.

Basically, most men have a codependent relationship with a moron. In order to avoid the pitfalls of having a dick, you have to ask yourself one key question:

*Do I have my dick in check?*

In a perfect world, your dick is the soldier, and you are Eisenhower.

You come up with the plan, and then your dick takes the beach.

But you have to oversee the operation the entire time. That's the secret: make your dick report to you, not the other way around.

"Hey, there's a hot blonde working over in human resources," your dick tells you. "She just broke up with her boy-friend and seems vulnerable."

"Thanks for the report, soldier. At ease."

At this point, you have to tell your dick to stand down while *you* devise a plan. Because if you let your dick do the planning, you'll probably wind up grabbing her ass in the company cafeteria and getting the shit slapped out of you.

Your dick has a *goal,* but it has no plan. And that's how men of astounding achievement can make the same mistake in the White House that you can make at a White Castle.

## When It Gets Hard, Get Smart!

When you want to bang someone on the side, come up with a strategy first. Then examine the approach and decide if it's doable or if it's a suicide mission. (We give you the basic tools in chapter 3, "The Blueprint.")

But sometimes your dick's impulses are overwhelming, and it starts telling you to take a chance. When you notice your dick getting too wise, rub one out first, and *then* begin the planning. For the love of God, don't sit there with heavy nuts and try to come up with a course of action. You're gonna end up looking as dumb as Mike Ditka when he traded his entire draft, put on a wig, and picked Ricky Williams.

Now that we've bashed having a dick, let's give your dick some props. Your dick is right way more than it's ever been given credit for. Every once in a while you should go out and, in a safe way, have some fun with a hottie. Remember: there's nothing wrong with that. Ignore the guilt trip that has been hyped in America for the last couple hundred years.

Hey, in France, having a mistress is considered completely normal. The exact thing that is damned to no end in this country is not looked down upon there. And guess what? The French people are not overrun with lustful thoughts. They get up in the morning, go to work, earn a living, and enjoy some side action on occasion. No big deal.

If all of this seems confusing, don't worry. Continue reading, learn the tricks of the trade, and always remember that you are the supreme Allied commander of your shlong.

# TRUE CHEAT

**Account by Anthony Cumia, radio personality,**
*The Opie and Anthony Show*
**Outcome:** *fail*

This is an epic fail story. I guess it was about 2008. I was going out with this fuckin' hot girl who worked in the industry here in New York. I don't know how I even scored her; it must have been my thrilling personality. We went out together for an entire summer. The girl was great arm candy; people were like, "Holy shit!"

I don't know why I needed to fuck this up, but . . .

Summer was winding down. We had just gotten back from the Bahamas. We had a great time, sex was great. She wanted to have an end-of-summer party at my house. She was planning this thing for a few weeks, and in the interim, I started chitchatting with a girl on one of the many Internet venues for picking up broads. She was really my type and everything, and I wanted to fuck her. *I wanted to fuck this girl!* Even though I had a hot girlfriend, I needed someone new to fuck.

Now, this girl I met on the Internet lived in Canada, but we had friends in common—as luck would have it, friends who were coming to this end-of-summer party. So I had her fly in so that they could bring her along. Bad idea, right from the start, I know it. You never invite the girl you're gonna cheat with to the same party that your girlfriend is at with you, at your house.

So now this girl, a hot blonde, is at the party, and I can't stop looking at her because all I can think about is how badly I want to fuck her, and my girlfriend is starting to notice that I'm not really paying attention to her. I am the worst when it comes to cheating, because I have no "cheat face" or game. I'll just be like, "Hey, I don't wanna fuck you anymore; I wanna fuck this girl." I can't lie.

I'm in the Jacuzzi with this girl, and my girlfriend is hanging out with my family and shit, but she's keeping an eye on me. And Blondie starts rubbing my leg in the hot tub—there's bubbles, so you can't see or anything, but I know that shit is gonna go down. I had been drinking throughout the course of the party and now was at the point where I just wanted to fuck this girl, and I didn't care about my relationship anymore or anything.

Toward the end of the party, when most people had left, I guess I was really being a little too touchy-feely with the Canadian girl. Well, my girlfriend saw it, got pissed, and left. And I'm like, "Cool." (I am the worst piece of shit!)

I take this girl up to my bedroom, we have great sex, and then fall asleep. The next morning, I get woken up by someone calling my name and knocking loudly on my bedroom door, which, thank God, I had locked. It was my girlfriend. I'm in bed with this other girl, and there's no way out, because my bedroom is on the second floor and has only the one door.

A la *Love, American Style*, I tell the girl to hide in the closet. I have two walk-in closets, one his and one hers, and "Hers" is full of all my girlfriend's stuff. So the blonde scrambles into the closet just as I open the bedroom door and say, in a groggy, sleepy voice, "Oh, hi, yeah, I'm just tired. I was sleeping."

My girlfriend starts giving me shit about my talking to the other girl at the party. She's looking around the room, and she must've just smelled the sex, because she demands, "Is she here?" And, of course, I lie like a motherfucker: "No! No!" She walks over and opens closet B—the one the girl wasn't in—looks inside, and then shuts the door and walks away. I'm thinking, "Oh my God, she looked in only one closet. I'm off scot-free! This is great!"

She's still lacing into me about how I made her look like an asshole the night before, which I did, and how I'm a fucking scumbag, which I am. Everything she was saying was right. Then she says, "What about this closet?" and throws open the door to find the blonde just standing there. Thank God she at least got some of her clothes on. "Hi," she says to my girlfriend.

"How long have you been fucking my boyfriend?"

"About two weeks."

That's when my girlfriend leaves my house, but not before taking my laptop computers, my keys, my Escalade, my pistol license. And I'm naked; I can't just run after her.

She wouldn't give any of my shit back for like two weeks, until I finally had a cop go over there to get it. That was pretty much the end of our relationship. That was my summer of the Canadian in the closet.

## The Fuckup

Wow. Let us begin by saying we're dumbfounded that Anthony not only believed that hiding the broad in the closet was somehow going to work, but also that his girlfriend actually knew he'd try to pull off a stunt like that. If you were standing next to his girlfriend when this happened and she said to you, "I bet this shit hid her in the closet," you'd say,

"That's the worst idea I've ever heard." And you'd both be right!

This brings us to Anthony's first mistake. Well, actually, this brings us to his *last* mistake, but let's work backward. Cumia took for granted how familiar his girl was with his horseshit. Think about it: in a blind, suspicious fury, she enters his home, knocks on his bedroom door, and he answers, giving the standard "I was just sleeping" routine.

Here's where most women, in a moment of introspection, would think, "Oh my God. I'm overreacting like a psycho." But this chick didn't buy his song and dance for a second. Within moments, she was in the room, opening the closet door, and finding the mark. Anthony's ball and chain was on to him, and no amount of lies or acting was going to throw her off the trail. We're sure he tried his best. Aside from the sleeping bit, when Anthony greeted his lady, he probably even gave her a look as if to say, "What the fuck are you doing here? Are you crazy?"

This look would have been justified completely, because what the fuck *was* she doing there?! Every man who is in the business of cheating needs his home to be a Fortress of Solitude. That means you protect your sanctum from being violated by suspicious girlfriends with moat, armed guard, security system, or eyeball scanner. So there's another mistake: he let down his guard.

Finally, Ant's initial blunder falls under the umbrellas of greed and impatience. Cumia was dating a chick who was on television in addition to being smoking hot, yet he needed to have more on the side. Greedy. The "other woman" lived in Canada, and Ant couldn't wait for their paths to cross, so he flew her in. Impatient. And, as noted in the story, Ant made his move at his house, at a party, in his hot tub, in front of his girlfriend. And his girlfriend had spent weeks planning the party! For fuck's sake. Greedy and impatient? Let's throw heartless in there too.

Always remember, there's a difference between doing what you need to do on the side and being greedy. If you have a good thing going, try to recognize it and appreciate it. There are several ways to define "a good thing." Way at the top of the list would be "hot girl who makes good cash, plans killer parties, and fucks really well."

Now let's talk about flying in pussy. Unless it's the mother of your children, don't do it. Okay, if you're Donald Trump, fine. But if you grew up on Long Island, where Anthony did, just wait until you find a drunken skank in a bar. Airfare tail is problematic.

First, it's expensive. If you want to pay for ass that badly, go get a hooker. Wait, we know what you're thinking: "But what if my faraway love turns out to be my future bride?" What are you, an asshole? The chances of that happening are as likely as you not regretting the eight hundred bucks you dropped on airfare the minute you drop your nut.

Second, if the broad lives far enough away to warrant your flying her in, you don't really know her or what you're getting into. A circumstance like this can set the stage for your new lady friend arriving as a dream girl and leaving as one of the biggest mistakes of your life. What if she turns out to be a total wing nut? What are you going to do then? You can't get rid of her, even if she's not staying with you. (We *really* hope that you didn't put her up in a hotel. What are you, made of money? Besides, any long-distance cheat who agrees to be stashed in a hotel for a week while you crash at home is *definitely* a wing nut.) She's still going to be up your ass for the duration of her stay, and you're stuck with her. You flew her in.

We don't even need to analyze the whole "making a move in the Jacuzzi at your girlfriend's party" thing. Even a prehistoric troglodyte found frozen in the earth and somehow thawed out and brought back to life would know why you don't do shit like that.

Congratulations, Ant. Scientists are going to have to invent a new class of caveman that will consist only of you. We hope you're proud of yourself. Seriously. This was a real achievement.

# Chapter 3

# The Blueprint

*The Who, What, When, Where, Why, and How*

Although a man can get involved in a variety of affairs, some general rules apply to just about every one of them. Throughout this book, we'll delve into the intricacies of the guidelines, practices, and principles of dealing with each. However, before we go any further, it's essential that you have a working knowledge of the basics, so here's the who, what, when, where, why, and how of cheating. Literally.

## How?

There's only one way to act when you're pulling off some sneaky shit like this, and that's to act like a sneak. Being discreet in all areas of a cheat is crucial. No matter what's prompting you to do it, or how excited and invigorated you may feel, or how high the risk or reward is, you keep your mouth shut and your ass covered. If you're asking "Why do I have to act so prudently when I cheat?" slap yourself across the face and get your shit together before you consider having an affair of any sort. Think about it: you're on the verge of doing something that could destroy not only your life, but also the lives of those around you. Even the tiniest slip-up can lead to utter catastrophe. Once there's a crack in the dam, the flood is on its way.

## Why?

Well, only you know the reason. Everybody is different. But you must figure out what kind of cheater you are. Maybe you're doing it for the rush. Maybe you're doing it for romance. Maybe you're cheating for a bit of extra passion in your life. Or maybe you're just a piece of shit. Now, keep in mind, there can be *poor* motives for stepping out: insecurity, revenge, assuming that your girl is cheating on you. Take a moment to ask yourself a few very important questions: Why am I cheating? Why do I want to bang this other woman? Why is the desire to have some strange lady touch my prick overtaking my life?

Your answer could be anything, such as: (a) you're trying to bury the shitty feelings from your crappy childhood; (b) you're lonely and need some extra affection; or (c) it just feels good to have some strange lady touch your prick. Some reasons are good, and some reasons are bad. The determining factor is this: if you truly understand who you are and why you're doing what you're doing, you're good to go.

Once you realize why you want to cheat and what you want to get out of it, you'll be able to deal with any consequences that may come down the pike. Answering the "why" question rationally and honestly will allow you to decipher the difference between a solid motive and a questionable one, which will, in turn, allow you to be in control. Always be in control. You are the master of your pussy domain. There's no screaming "It's not my fault!" when it comes to cheating.

## Who?

This is a big one, and, once again, it revolves around keeping a low profile. There's a simple rule to follow here: *never fuck a liability*. If the mark is in close proximity to your or your girl's daily life, don't do it. You're already taking enough of a gamble without burdening yourself with any of that other bullshit too. Always go for the mark or the pro who can easily be kept at bay or who truly understands and respects your situation. Don't get tangled up with a chick who has immediate high expectations of you. In fact, even if these expectations don't exist at the beginning of an affair, there's a high probability they will develop in time. A girl, at some point, will most likely have strong desires to meet your family, to know your friends, to spend the holidays with you, or ask to swing by your workplace "just to say hi." It's at this point—or, ideally, before this point—that you tell her to beat it. In the nicest possible way, of course.

## Where?

When it comes to picking out a location to conduct your filth, you need to think like a criminal who doesn't want to get caught. If you planned to rob a bank—no, we're not condoning robbery, we're just making a funny analogy, you Goodie Two-shoes—you'd think about the pre- and post-logistics before you even worried about how to crack the vault.

First off, you need to avoid as many witnesses as possible. You don't want to find yourself surrounded by a bunch of potential bigmouths. If this *were* a bank robbery and one of the tellers identified your face, you'd have to shoot him. But then if another teller saw you do that, you'd have to shoot *her*. Finally, everybody's dead, the cops have you surrounded, and you have to blow your brains out. Anyway, the point is, if you have a doorman, a nosey neighbor, a roommate, etc., you're going to have to figure out how to elude them. You can't assume that they'll lie for you. They might feel guilty and not want to be involved. But even if they're willing to comply, the more people you fold into your scheme, the worse everything gets. People fuck up royally trying to lie for themselves, let alone trying to remember the details of *your* shit life. Taking the mark to your place will also require an intensive cleanup, to make sure she hasn't left behind anything that could get you burned.

Ideally, you're better off going to her house or apartment: no cleanup, and you won't need to give a fuck about her neighbors. A hotel works too, although that may bring curious credit card charges. Even if you pay in cash, most places require placing a temporary hold on your credit card upon check-in. Since you'll have to shower after sex—*always, without exception*—your skin will have the scent of strange soaps. We know guys who have gotten caught for smelling like a cheap facial bar.

An even safer bet is a car, preferably hers. Again, no cleanup necessary. Since a shower will be out of the question, we don't suggest full-on fucking in the vehicle, but a little heavy petting or receiving some oral is usually fine. Obviously, you need to find a safe, secluded spot to park where you don't have to worry about a cop shining his flashlight through the windshield. Don't get blown while parked at the mall. Find an alley, industrial park, or quiet street, for Christ's sake.

## When?

As far as the time of day is concerned, be Dracula. Nighttime is always better to cheat. More people are out during the day: driving to work, walking to lunch, sitting in traffic. Holy scissors, there are children playing in parks. But at night, things go quiet. The kids are tucked away, the birds are asleep, and the sun is on the other side of the planet. It will be much harder for someone to recognize you at night. The darkness allows you to slowly and safely slip out of your vampire's coffin. Still, what if you (or your mark) work the overnight at some hospital or gas station? Well, there are detrimental factors and convenient circumstances at any given hour, depending on your lifestyle and schedule.

When is good for you? What is that perfect time of day when you can go sight unseen and have enough time after sex to get rid of any and every incriminating clue? Whenever you do your dirty work, just make sure you have the time to do it right. The weightier "when" question is the more philosophical one: when are you mentally prepared to do this? The answer will come only after you've intimately familiarized your filthy self with every nook, cranny, and crevice of this despicable book.

Good luck, and Godspeed.

# TRUE CHEAT

**Account by Robert Kelly, comedian, actor, coauthor of this book**

**Outcome:** *fail*

I was eighteen and working at Grossman's Bargain Outlet, which was a shitty lumber store that sold warped two-by-fours and messed-up indoor/outdoor carpet with holes in it. I was the king of it. I was at the top of my game back then. I was shredded, I was gorgeous, I had a fuckin' curly mullet and abs. Oh my God, I used to bang a lot of chicks.

A guy, who for legal reasons I'll call Ron, had just gotten out of the army reserves and came back to our store for a week to train for a management position at another location. He had been "me" before I got there: the cool guy who got all the chicks. But now he wasn't that cool guy anymore. He was a little chunky, a little more serious, a little more mature.

Ron was engaged to a girl he'd been with for the last couple of years. Before he left us for the other store, he told me that he'd just gotten his fiancée a cashier job at Grossman's. Poor move. You never wanna get your chick a job where you work and then leave to go somewhere else.

So his fiancée came in, and she was gorgeous. She was a typical Boston chick back in the early nineties: big, big, big hair; tight jeans; fluorescent fuckin' tank tops; tanning-bed tan; beautifully manicured nails. A *Jersey Shore* type of chick. I took one look and was like, "Holy shit!" In hindsight, I don't know if she was *really* that hot or if it was because I worked at shitty Grossman's Bargain Outlet, and hot chicks didn't go there. In the real world, she might have been a fuckin' 4.5, but at fuckin' Grossman's Bargain Outlet, this bitch was a 10.

My boss, who was also a creep, saw me looking at her while I was fixing some Electrolux vacuum cleaner in an aisle or something. I was just staring at her like a fuckin' wolf waiting to scavenge a bear's leftover meat as soon as it leaves. He sidled up to me and whispered, "You'll never get that. She'll never go out with a guy like you. Don't even think about it." To me, it was a challenge. Really? I'll get whatever the fuck I want.

So I flirted with her, made her laugh, treated her like a gentleman would, and invited her upstairs to this shitty room I had set up as my "office," although it was more like a tree fort in the attic. We had lunch, I made her laugh some more, and then I did that Prince shit from *Purple Rain*, the way he stares at Apollonia.

Ron's fiancée picked up on the vibe between us. "What are you doing?" she said, just as I moved in for the kiss—and she fuckin' went for it. Then there was the moment of "We shouldn't do this." "I know, I know."

I invited her out that night. I didn't think she was gonna call me, but she did. I took her to "my spot" over by the water, where the waves crash over the car at certain times of the night, depending on the tide. It was like *From Here to Eternity*, except in a shitty Honda. I fuckin' went all out. I ate her pussy, I ate her asshole, I did everything that I knew Ron wasn't doing anymore. And she flipped out. I made her cum like ten times. She blew me, I pulled her hair, I choked her a little bit. The little creepy shit? She loved it. What a freak.

She broke off her engagement to Ron that week, all because I'd flipped her out so bad. We wound up going out for years. We fell in love; everything was beautiful. And then all of a sudden, things became routine, and we wound up not having sex like we used to anymore and just eating every day. I remember one time we were sitting under a tree on a 100-degree day, eating tuna melts and a small pizza, and we just fell asleep like two fat buffalo.

One day she said to me out of the blue, "I need a change. I'm thinking of going to college."

I was like, "Oh, fuck me." So she winds up going to college. A *real* college, not a fuckin' community college like where I was going, which was like high school. She was actually gonna learn shit and get a degree.

All of a sudden she wasn't laughing at me as much. She was on a diet, and out of the blue, "Tuna melts are bad for you." Me? I was still eating like a fuckin' savage. I knew something was off, and one day my instincts kicked in. I just knew something was up. While she was in the bathroom, I went through her purse, and I found a piece of paper with the name Scott and a phone number on it.

When she came out, I held up the piece of paper and asked, "Who's this?"

"Oh, that's my cousin Scott." She said it so innocently and convincingly.

But not *that* convincingly. Although I backed off, pretending to believe her, I *knew* that wasn't true. I fuckin' knew it! It's not like I could take her to court, though. There's no fuckin' "Cheat Court."

A week later, I was sitting in an AA meeting, trying to get "spiritual," and I just couldn't stop thinking about it. So I said, "Fuck it." I went to her house, asked her to come outside, and we sat on her stoop for two hours. I just kept repeating, "Tell me. Just tell me." She kept insisting that she had nothing to tell. "You're crazy! What are you talking about?" But I guess I wore her down. Finally, she took a deep breath and admitted, "Okay. Scott is a hockey player . . ." And I said, "Fuck me! She's fucking the hockey player." (If you're out there, Scott, fuck you.)

She was fucking Scott because he was fresh and new and exciting. She was trading up. She was trading in her lease on me—a rusty old hatchback—for a brand-new Honda. *Just like she had done to Ron.* I was the new Ron: fat and lonely, with nobody.

After two weeks of writing poetry and being sad, I went on a tear. From then on, I cheated on every girl I was ever with. I cheated on them before they cheated on me, because I knew that *someone* was gonna cheat. So it might as well be me before I got fuckin' crushed again. This one relationship was the catalyst for sending me down a path of being a fuckin' total creep, sexual deviant, cheating motherfucker.

That finally came to an end twenty years later, when I got caught cheating by the woman that I still love today. Everything came crashing down, and I hit bottom. It was either lose everything that I had with my girl or try to not be a scumbag. And I made the choice to try.

You know, not to cheat.

## The Fuckup

This is such a great story because it incorporates so many important life lessons in being both the cheat and the sap in the relationship.

Let's begin with the most important detail: Bobby Kelly

knowingly entered a relationship with a woman who began the courtship while she was engaged to someone else.

Sometimes in life, the answer is so obvious that you don't even see it. You wouldn't think that someone would have to tell you to never go out with someone who is cheating on someone else with you. Right out of the gate, this person is showing you exactly who she is. If you met some chick for the first time while she was poaching bear claws, would you sign over your power of attorney? If you saw a homeless man eating out of a garbage can, would you let him watch your parakeet? Then why the fuck would you get into a committed relationship with a known cheat? It's simple: the male ego knows no limits.

The rush of seducing someone who is already in a relationship is that it makes you feel like Count fuckin' Dracula. Try it out sometime. You could be a high school dropout working at Starbucks, but mentally you'll feel like you're wearing a cape with your shit slicked back. If you're not careful, you'll start talking with a Transylvanian accent.

But it's all bullshit. She's not cheating *because* of you, she's cheating because she's just *like* you. She's a dirtbag. (On *Dr. Phil,* the "experts" would probably say it's because she got molested or that her dad left when she was only six. But don't listen to them. We have a hunch they're simply pandering to their audience in order to keep their ratings high enough to afford flashy cars so that they can go bang some whores.)

Bobby's mistake was that he gave his heart to a heartless woman. What he should have done was show the world what a pig this girl was and moved on with his life. This isn't the type of woman you get serious with. It's the kind of girl you use to ensure that you never have a midlife crisis. Every filthy thing you can think of, you do with a woman like this.

Then twenty years down the road, if you ever think to yourself, "Oh man, I never . . ." you immediately remember, "Wait! Yes I did! With that cheating slut from the lumber-yard." Then you can spend the rest of your day tossing the football to your hypothetical son, with the peace of mind that comes only from having eaten out a girl's ass in a shitty Honda Civic while the ocean crashes over you.

The second lesson in this sad tale is to never take your foot off the hammer in your relationship. Women are just like us. Consciously or unconsciously, they are always looking for something better. Even good girls will look for something better *if you give them a reason.*

It's extremely important to keep your sex life going. If you get tired of fucking your woman, she's going to go find someone who is a little more motivated. So every once in a while, even if you truly love your wife or girlfriend, you have to throw her facedown in the pillows and treat her like you don't know her.

What's that? "No, she's special. I could never do that to her."

Bullshit! Put her to sleep before someone else does. It'll keep her honest.

If she doesn't feel special around you, every day she leaves the house, she'll be showing a little more skin. And next thing you know, every caped dude she works with will be slicking back his hair and popping his head over the cu-bicle divider, saying, "Good *eeeevening.*"

In conclusion: ol' sadomasochistic Bobby gives as good as he gets. For some reason, Bobby didn't realize that he and his predecessor Ron were the same person. But that's why you've got to love him. Bobby will always hang around long enough to get burned by the stove that he turned on. He's like the crook who returns to the crime scene and starts pestering the cops, "Hey, you guys got any leads?" Even though he was young, he deserved every bit of the heartache he endured. And if it makes you feel any better, Robert, we're sure that Scott the hockey player suffered a similar fate.

# Chapter 4

# What Kind of Scumbag Are You?

*Cheater Profiles*

Cheaters are a hard bunch to stereotype. They're quite a diverse lot. A two-timer isn't always going to be some fast-talker with oily hair and a cheap suit, or an orange-tanned, beach-bodied douche bag who likes to talk about his six-pack. We've categorized the nine basic types of scumbags so that you can identify your own strengths and weaknesses.

## Cheater Class 1: The Accidental Tourist

**MO:** a guy who cheats unintentionally due to the influence of alcohol or controlled substances. He truly didn't mean to do it.

**Odds of Getting Caught:** probable. His overwhelming guilt will lead him to behave suspiciously, which will prompt an interrogation, which will draw out a confession.

## Cheater Class 2: The Rookie

**MO:** stiff, straightlaced, neurotic, and obsessively organized. Attempts at cheating are sabotaged by overplanning and too much attention to detail.

**Odds of Getting Caught:** high. While thoroughness is a useful tool, being suave is instrumental. If you can't be cool during a cheat, mistakes will be made.

## Cheater Class 3: The Addict

**MO:** lack of childhood family structure and proper upbringing have led to relentless cheating on every woman he's ever been with. Translation: he'll bang anything, anywhere, anytime.

**Odds of Getting Caught:** definite. Because of his sloppy preparation and execution, the bottom is inevitable.

## Cheater Class 4: The Undercover Cop

**MO:** very private. He definitely cheats; he just tries to appear faithful, and mostly succeeds. His friends know he does it, and he knows he does it. But he'll die before he admits it.

**Odds of Getting Caught:** low. You could waterboard him for days, but he'd never talk.

**Be forewarned:** *the Undercover Cop's approach also makes him believe that he's morally superior to the average cheater. Bullshit.*

## Cheater Class 5: The Defensive Offensive

**MO:** a man who cheats out of sheer panic. His girlfriend doesn't call him back quickly enough, so his insecurity convinces him that she's cheating on him. He then cheats frantically in retaliation.

**Odds of Getting Caught:** almost definite. This guy is like a cop who shoots somebody because he thinks the hairbrush they're holding is a pistol.

**Be forewarned:** *this is the most dangerous type of cheater. Never cheat without a strategy.*

## Cheater Class 6: The Artist

**MO:** pretends to have an interest in exploring his creative side so that he can take a course in painting, pottery, or acting— and then try to bang the girls in it.

**Odds of Getting Caught:** fairly low, as long as he's willing to talk to his wife/girlfriend at length about how the classes are helping him "grow and discover."

## Cheater Class 7: The Codependent

**MO:** loves to fuck around, but has no concept of independence or self-reliance. Ashamed of his infidelity, he charmingly drags his pals into his predicament so that he can feel the comfort of being surrounded by fellow sinners. Talks a lot about "the team," but is out only for himself.

**Odds of Getting Caught:** not only is he going to get popped, he's going to bring down everyone else with him.

**Be forewarned:** *stay away from this guy. No matter how much fun he seems to be, he is not your friend.*

## Cheater Class 8: The Serial Killer

**MO:** the demon with the million-dollar smile. A clergyman, senator, family man, or other likable asshole who cons you into believing that he's as wholesome as a park picnic. Meanwhile, he's sharpening his cock the whole time.

**Odds of Getting Caught:** extremely low, since he's not a likely suspect. However, if the shit goes down for this guy, the backlash will be newsworthy.

**Be forewarned:** *this type of cheater feels compelled to collect potentially incriminating mementos from his mark (nude photos, dirty letters/emails, etc.) and then leave these items in relatively easy-to-find places—almost like he wants to get caught.*

## Cheater Class 9: The Rock Star

**MO:** good-looking, powerful, and unstoppable with women. Has a high sex drive, very few ethics, and zero remorse. He is able to charm his way in and out of any situation. This is the Teflon Don.

**Odds of Getting Caught:** impossible. Even his girlfriend/wife will be blinded by his charisma, never suspecting that he'd deceive her.

## CHEATER PROFILES QUIZ

From what you've just read, you now know that cheaters come in all shapes and sizes. Understanding what breed of dog you are and what other kinds of dogs are out there will only facilitate your success in scoring side snatch.

**1. If you believe that when you cheated it truly wasn't your fault and/or your own doing, you're:**

(a) insane.

(b) an idiot.

(c) a child.

(d) the Accidental Tourist.

**2. The Codependent is great to hang around with because:**

(a) he gets you a lot of puss.

(b) he's great for a laugh.

(c) both A and B.

(d) he's *never* great to hang with. Stay away from this asshole.

**3. Another name for the Serial Killer could be:**

(a) Tiger Woods.

(b) the famous black guy who plays professional golf.

(c) the guy who, as a two-year-old kid, outputted comedian Bob Hope on *The Mike Douglas Show* in 1978.

(d) Eldrick Tont Woods, aka Tiger.

**4. You know you're a Rock Star if you:**

(a) got pinched only once, but it was because you felt like it.

(b) never got pinched, but secretly want to because this cheating shit is getting out of hand.

(c) retired your jersey at long last after banging every single type of broad you could possibly imagine.

(d) finally stopped cheating—with a record of zero convictions—but only because you died.

**5. If you want to easily justify your selfish infidelity, the best type of cheater to be is:**

(a) an Addict. After all, you're doing it only because of the way you were raised.

(b) an Undercover Cop. After all, it's not like you're flaunting it or anything.

(c) a Defensive Offensive. After all, a guy needs to stand up for himself.

(d) the Artist. After all, at least you're learning while you do it.

# Chapter 5

# Choosing a Mark

*Who to Fuck, Who to Flee*

We're friends with a retired police officer. One of us came up with a scheme for a perfect murder and asked him about it.

This is as far as we got:

"Okay, me and a friend of mine—"

"Stop!" the cop interrupted. "You're already caught. The second you involve another person in your plan, you're done. Because somebody is gonna fuck up, and when that somebody gets questioned and begins to think about life in prison, he's gonna try to cut a deal. And guess whose name he's gonna give to the cops? The best way to commit a murder is to do it yourself. And if you want the highest odds of not getting caught, kill some random person that you have no connection to."

So, applying that theory: when you're going to cheat, it's best to do it with someone who isn't in your social or professional circles. You don't want your cheat to know anyone who knows your real girl, or your drinking buddies, or your coworkers. And after you bang her, keep your fucking mouth shut.

However, keeping your mouth shut is not a strong suit for men *or* women. The stereotypes are that women run their yaps and guys can keep a secret. That's bullshit. For 99 percent of human beings, "Don't tell anyone" means "Tell only your best friend."

And guess what?

That second wave will run and tell his or her best friend, and so on and so on. Eventually everybody is going to know except for your girlfriend or wife. And at that point, it's only a matter of time before the whole thing blows up in your face.

As a man in a relationship, you must acknowledge the immense power that you hand a cheat the second you bang her. Her ability to completely fuck over your life does not exist until you fuck her. But having a dick never seems to allow most men the luxury of contemplating this fact until *after* they've done the deed.

You can minimize your risk by choosing the right mark. Here is a long list of classic cheats that have sent many a man up the river. In case there is any confusion, we're telling you who to cheat with by showing you who to *stay away* from.

# The Chick at Work

You know the type. She comes to work every day. She looks good. She smells good. And you're already rubbing one out to her anyway, so why not throw her down on the desk, right? Wrong!

Nothing gets a guy caught quicker than fucking some girl he works with. First of all, everyone is going to know that you're fucking her. We don't know why. We don't know how. But something happens the second you become intimate with another human being.

Is it the way the two of you stand when you talk to each other? Is it the amount of eye contact? Who knows?

Even if you have a nice long conversation with your cheat about how the two of you are going to play it cool and professional at work and act as if nothing happened, people are still going to figure it out.

Even if you can avoid that inevitability, it will eventually dawn on you that if this girl wants to, she can call your girlfriend and tell her everything. Fuck! Now you have to be nice to her. Every time your real girlfriend goes to the office picnic, this other girl could pull the trigger. What if she has a couple of drinks and decides to spill the beans in front of the entire company?

It's a fucking nightmare and is not worth it. Don't shit where you eat. You have to respect your career. You have to respect the fact that as a man, most of your self-worth is based on your ability to earn a living. The last thing you want to do is put some skank in the driver's seat of your ability to go to work and focus on your job.

*Do not fuck anybody you work with*. Stop being so goddamn lazy. Go out to a bar, hit on some random chick, fuck her, shower, and then go home and act like it never happened. If the president can get caught banging some chick at work, how do you think *you're* going to make out?

## The Chick at the Gym

She is not nearly as dangerous as the chick at work. But you should avoid cheating with the chick at the gym simply because you are definitely going to see her again. Seeing someone you fucked again and again creates a relationship due to proximity.

Once you've fucked her, now you have to say hi to her. If you don't, you risk pissing her off and then having her ask questions about your life. What do you think will happen when she finds out you're in a relationship? She's going to feel cheap and want to exact some form of revenge. You don't want to figure out what that entails.

Then, what if your girlfriend or wife decides that it would be smarter for the two of you to go to the same gym? Now you either have to do some fast talking to your cheat ("I met someone special five minutes ago—see ya!") or you have to finesse your real woman ("Well, gym time is my 'me' time. It's where I get out all the stress of the day, so I can come home to *you,* baby"). Trust us, all either woman will hear is: "I'm fucking someone else."

Another variable is the turnover at the gym. The possibility of someone you know, someone your girl knows, or simply someone you work with joining the gym is relatively high. Think about it: do you want the human evidence of your lack of loyalty striking up a conversation with your girlfriend or some chick who knows your girlfriend?

You can't get away from the smoking gun. If you do make this move, immediately exercise damage control. Cancel your membership and join another gym. For your sake, we hope you didn't sign up with Bally, because those motherfuckers *never* let you leave.

## Your Girlfriend's Roommate or Best Friend

You are probably thinking, "Jesus Christ, this one is pretty obvious." Well, never underestimate the stupidity of a horny man—or the depths to which a fucked-up woman will descend.

The obvious aspects are as follows: *guys listen to their dicks.* And a lot of us think that just about every female out there wants to bang us. Hence, we let our ego run with this idea. Then we have a couple of drinks. Next thing you know, we are making a pass at our girlfriend's best friend, while our real woman is ordering an appetizer.

*Don't ever make this move.* The rate of survival is slightly above that of a suicide bomber. The only reason to ever pull a move like this is because you simply don't have the balls to break up with your girlfriend. Banging someone this close to her is a guarantee that she'll find out and dump you first—possibly in a shallow grave.

But when a guy tries to bang his woman's girlfriend or roommate, it isn't always 100 percent his fault. A segment of the female population gets off on banging their friend's man—or at the very least, trying to turn him on. (We know that if we ever made that statement on *The View,* we'd get booed out of the building. No woman denies in a one-on-one conversation that sluts exist. But if you get them in a group, they turn into some sort of corporation that has to toe the company line: "No known evidence of whores amongst women.")

The reality is that the same way that there are a bunch of fucked-up men out there, there are also a bunch of fucked-up women. Honestly, how many times have you gone over to your girlfriend's apartment, and her roommate walks out of her room dressed in an outfit skimpy enough to make your dick hard, yet modest enough to make your girlfriend look like a psycho if she objects?

We aren't women, nor are we psychologists, so all we can do is take a guess as to what this kind of female is about. Women can get a lot in life simply by being desired, and that means there is a competition among women for a man's attention.

Some women fear the day they lose the ability to make a man stammer and suddenly have to hold their own through their personality and ability to produce. Others get off on being able to seduce a man who is already in a relationship. These are the *Fatal Attraction*–type chicks you want absolutely nothing to do with.

To be fair to the opposite sex, sometimes your male ego seizes command of your brain and distorts your perception. "She's wearing that revealing outfit for me. She wants to fuck!" But other times, you're actually right: the friend or roomie *is* trying to turn you on. And she *will* fuck you if you're dumb enough to do it.

Stay the fuck away from this kind of woman. You ever

hear those girls who call into *Loveline* and whine about how their dads didn't stick around, or how they got touched funny when they were kids, and now they have all these sexual-boundary issues? Those women have to live somewhere, right? That could even mean living with the girl you're going out with.

After you have a sexual run-in with one of these psychos, their first move will be to feel guilty and clear the air with your girlfriend. Somehow it will all end up being your fault. Your relationship is going to blow up, and underneath it all, the psycho roommate will feel some sort of hotness victory. It's fucked!

Be aware of how weak we men are. Step outside your horniness and ego and learn to recognize when you are in one of these situations. Then go home and rub one out to her memory instead.

## Married Women

This is kind of a wild card. The safety of this situation is that the female has as much to lose as you do if anyone finds out. Therefore, you can usually count on your partner in crime to keep her mouth shut. But here's the eight-hundred-pound gorilla in the room: she's *married*. Every time you send a text message, you have to worry about whether she left her phone sitting on the coffee table and her husband happens to be sitting there. What if he then glances down and reads your perverted text message?

There's already enough stress in cheating. The last thing you want to do is to be banging some broad, worried that, at any second, her husband is going to burst into the room and shoot her through your back. (We know, that's a fucked-up visual.)

We're just trying to help you understand the magnitude of the situation you're getting yourself into. Stay away from the married broads. Stick with the divorcées.

## Your Neighbor

This is obviously a huge fucking mistake. You don't need an angry or aggressive mark living downstairs, upstairs, next door, or across the way. She will either want to see you more or be pissed that you've cut things off. The next thing you know, she's bringing over a plate of homemade brownies at a time when she *knows* your girl is home. "Hi! I just wanted to introduce myself!" Then she's inside your house, and every time your girl leaves the room, you're hissing through clenched teeth, "I *told* you never to come here uninvited. Are you *crazy*?!"

And what if it's a neighbor you and your girlfriend both knew *before* you started sleeping with her? Uh-oh. Now the stage is set for the cheat to suddenly start dropping by more frequently and suggesting that you all get together on weekends. Eventually your woman wonders where this sudden spike in neighborly interest came from. Once she starts inquiring about that, it's only a matter of time before she comments, "I think our neighbor has a crush on you." And once *that* statement is on the table, it's a short hop to "Are you fucking her?!" So, for the love of God, *don't fuck your neighbor*. And that goes for the lady "down the street" too. Keep your secret pussy secret, as in "a few towns over," or at least in the next zip code.

## The Old Reliables

The safe women to cheat with are far less individually defin-able than the dangerous ones. The broads you should stay away from all share that common thread of being able to shatter your life in a heartbeat. Close proximity, professional and social ties, potential physical danger, or high emotional expectations and demands always serve as perfect ingredi-ents for disaster.

So who's a safe bet? It's not that complicated. As long as your cheat is single, not involved in your professional life, not a member of any club or social circle you belong to, not connected to your woman in any way, and doesn't live close by, you should be fine. It may sound like we've eliminated a large percentage of women from the pool of potentials. We haven't. In actuality, you've probably lost only about 23 percent of them. So go find and fuck one of the remaining 77 percent.

# WHO-NOT-TO-CHEAT-WITH QUIZ

In the interest of not intimidating you during the learning process, we're gonna lob the first couple of questions over the plate. After that, it's chin music. We're not fucking around.

**1. Which one of the following should you never, ever cheat with?**

(a) a coworker.

(b) a broad you met at the gym.

(c) a chick who is friends with your chick.

(d) all of the fucking above!

**2. Your buddy is going out of town, and he asks you to hang with his wife while he's gone. You know, just to keep her company. During a friendly encounter, she tells you that your buddy has been running around on her, and she's lonely, and she knows how to keep her mouth shut. What's your next move?**

(a) You respectfully decline, let her vent, then give her some comforting advice, helping her to realize that she's a beautiful person who's better than using cheap sex to compensate for her marital woes.

(b) You immediately call your friend to tell him that his wife is tossing her beaver at you.

(c) You bang her. Hey, why not? He's cheating on her, right?

(d) You have no clue what your next move would be in this situation, because you didn't even get as far as taking her out because you knew it was a terrible idea from the jump.

**3. At the office Christmas party, your boss's drunken wife pulls you into the copy room (oh, what a cliche) and offers to blow you while you sit**

**on the copy machine and it scans a picture of your balls. Your response should be:**

(a) "Absolutely! Fuck my boss. That guy's had a hard-on for me for years."

(b) "Are you out of your cotton-pickin' mind, you dizzy skirt?!"

(c) "I'd love to. You're gorgeous. But as much as we both want this, we know that tomorrow morning we'll appreciate our unrequited desires much more than the faint memory of a drunken fling."

(d) "I'm too afraid I'll get fired, so no. But, if you want, I'll perform cunnilingus on you while *you* sit on top of the copy machine. That way, the scanned pictures will be of your privates, not mine, thus allowing me to blackmail you if necessary and not vice versa."

**4. The new neighbor next door to you and your chick is hot, and she wants to bang you. You say no initially, but then she tells you that she's a high-priced prostitute, so it's cool—and on the house. You then:**

(a) say, "Abso-fucking-lutely! What could go wrong?! I'm dealin' with a pro!"

(b) report her to the police and rid yourself of any further temptation.

(c) wait until your chick's out of town and allow yourself a one-time-only indulgence.

(d) convince one of your single buddies to do it and tell you all about it.

**5. If you're going to cheat, it's always okay to do it with a woman who is:**

(a) divorced, independent, and not a member of your neighborhood book club.

(b) married, independent, and possibly looking to join your neighborhood book club.

(c) divorced, dependent, and the moderator of your neighborhood book club.

(d) married, dependent, but doesn't know how to read.

**Answer key:** (1) d, (2) d, (3) c, (4) d, (5) a.

# Chapter 6

# The Cleanup
## Destroying the Evidence

Depending on where you conduct your infidelity, there are certain postcoital custodial duties that need tending to. Cleanup is of dire importance. Sloppiness in this area gets a lot of guys pinched.

Most of this chapter is dedicated to the potential pitfalls of cheating in your own home, but boning in a motel room doesn't necessarily mean you're in the clear. The only fail-safe location is in the mark's apartment. Who gives a shit how big a mess you make there? It's not your problem.

There are two basic duties to complete after the deed is done. We even made them rhyme so that they're easy to remember.

# Take an Hour to Shower and Scour

Very few people get caught in the act of cheating. What usually does you in is sloppy cleanup. So after you've parted ways with your mark, getting away scot-free begins. This entire process should take you about an hour. Your head may be reeling a bit, as your balls are now empty and rational thought has begun to take over. Don't panic. Remain calm and focus on what you need to do. Just know that if you follow these steps, no one is going to suspect a thing.

*Shower*

First things first. Trash your underwear. It's probably going to look like you were hiding a Cinnabon in it, which would be a hilarious lie to tell, but it won't work. And don't throw it anywhere your girl might find it. Dumpsters and sewer grates are your friends. Now, you're going to want to scrub your body like you were just at a nuclear testing site, particularly your face, fingers, and balls, since those will be the three main locales of vagina stench. It is crucial that you give yourself adequate time to do this, so as to not encounter your better half while reeking of another woman's baby crack. You also need some time after the wash to smell natural again.

But you don't want to smell *too* fresh, like you just showered for no apparent reason. People who do that are always people who just did something really shitty. Don't worry, the second phase will allow time for the fresh scent to settle. Lastly, if you're showering at a motel, bring your own soap. Even the faint smell of motel soap is a red flag that you've been up to no good.

## Scour

Face it: you've just committed an act that some people find as despicable as murder. Cleaning is not enough. You need to scour your surroundings. This includes combing the environment for any stray hairs, Swiffering under all furniture for out-of-sight items, and eradicating any questionable stains, which means everything from lipstick on your collar to milk spots on the bed. Also, women love to leave behind little keepsakes. It's their way of saying "Miss you" and "Fuck you" at the same time. Upon meeting, examine the mark and make a mental note of any jewelry, bangles, or accessories that will be coming off at bang time. This is a worthwhile exercise, since there are a number of hazardous materials that she may, and probably will, "forget" to take with her (see the section on glitter below). Find these items and get rid of them, no matter how unimportant they seem. We don't give a shit if you find that watch the guy had up his ass in *Pulp Fiction*. It's gone.

Note: You can skip the scour step if the encounter takes place in a motel or such, unless your chick is staying there with you. In that case, clean this one twice. Those are close quarters, and she's bound to immediately spot something out of the ordinary.

## Potential Snares

### Scrunchies

Unless you're Fabio or the lead singer of an '80s hair metal band, it's going to be quite difficult justifying the discovery of a scrunchie. They're small and malleable, so they can easily slip between the couch cushions or get lodged under a bed pillow, but they're easy to spot. A quick scan of your environment will suffice for detecting these unwanted mementos.

## Hair Extensions

This one used to apply only to black chicks, so you didn't always have to worry about it. But these days, every broad is on the bandwagon. They all want Beyoncé hair. Even fundamentalist Muslim broads could have a few fake locks underneath their beekeeper hoods. Extensions are tough, because the girl might not always take them out on purpose, which means that you can't always monitor their whereabouts. Sometimes these damn things just fall out when you bang. Still, it's hard not to notice something that looks like a dead muskrat, regardless of where it lands.

## Contact Lens Case

If your girlfriend finds a lens case that was left behind, you can't lie about it, even if you or your girlfriend wears contacts. Your first instinct will be to say, "Oh, baby, I picked up an extra contact lens case. It can't hurt to have a spare." But that lie won't work because the goddamn thing is gonna be dirty as shit from sitting in the bottom of the other chick's purse.

## Bobby Pins

Fuck these things. Unlike the scrunchie, you can't always tell when a girl is wearing one of these cocksuckers. Bobby pins are often buried so deep in a woman's mane that it's like the government implanted them there. They're also hard to detect on any surface. Often, at first glance, the bobby pin may appear to be a small crack or hair. They're also great at hiding out in hard-to-find places for months at a time, only to be discovered and bite you in the ass long after you thought you were in the clear. So get on your hands and knees like a goddamn chambermaid and examine every thin black line you see. Yeah, it sucks, but so does your chick cutting the sleeves off all your shirts because she found something you thought was just a piece of string.

### The Lone Earring

This one isn't so bad. It's a favorite forget-me-not for most women, but because they actually care about jewelry, they'll never leave one of these out of sight. You'll always find the lone earring on the nightstand or dresser, since—although you've abandoned her—the broad's gonna want it back.

### Tampon/Tampon Wrapper

Trash cans are a bitch, since they're the last place you think to check. But make sure these do not go uninspected. A used tampon or the wrapper from one is an instant conviction. Trust us, your girl definitely knows if she has her period or not. Also, be sure to attend to any other discarded evidence, such as: packaging from food you never eat; bulk garbage that proves more than one person was hanging out; or something completely incriminating, like an empty lipstick or eyeliner case. You know what? The more we talk about it, the more we realize: just play it safe and empty all the trash cans.

And now for the whopper motherfucker of a potential snare:

*Glitter*

To a cheating man, there is no greater adversary, no better foil, no more formidable foe than glitter. Remember this: glitter is a motherfucker.

It sits there all pretty and shiny, sparkling, pretending to be innocent, while it silently plots to destroy your life. The goddamn son of a bitch bastard has ruined countless brilliantly planned cheats. Just as you're about to cross the finish line, blue ribbon within reach, unknowing girlfriend on the sidelines smiling and cheering you on, glitter swoops in with a lead pipe and shatters your kneecaps.

## GLITTER DETECTION

The problem with this shit is that it gets everywhere and clings relentlessly to every surface imaginable. Glitter is the all too wily, unmanageable *X* factor. You never know where it's going to turn up, so stay away from it. If the mark arrives looking like she just slid down a rainbow, *abort mission*! This may take her by surprise or come off as rude, but rest assured that you will suffer tenfold the heartache if you proceed.

## POTENTIAL EXCUSES

There aren't any. No dude you were hanging out with (or decent, upstanding woman) was wearing glitter. Those glistening flakes are reserved for sluts, strippers, and dingbats. In other words, chicks you're trying to bang on one level or another.

Again, stay away.

We repeat: *stay away.*

## WHY DO THEY WEAR IT?

Who the hell knows?

People have been enamored of glitter since the beginning of time. There are mica flakes in ancient cave paintings, for Christ's sake. Even in 40,000 BC, women wanted "shimmer." So this stuff isn't going anywhere anytime soon.

In 1934 a machinist from New Jersey named Henry Ruschmann invented the modern form of glitter by grinding up plastic. His company, Meadowbrook Inventions, still exists today. Its slogan: "Our Glitter Covers the World."

On behalf of the entire cheating community, fuck you, Henry Ruschmann, you cocksucker.

Most folks would say that women wear glitter because it's fun or sexy or enchanting. Nonsense. It's a woman's way of marking you. Once you've been branded by glitter's wicked burn, you're off-limits to all other women until you get that shiny shit off of you. It's the male version of the scarlet letter. And if you're still not convinced that it's a truly rotten substance, know that glitter is a persistent environmental pollutant because of its size and the fact that it's non-biodegradable.

So we hope you're proud, ladies. Wearing it means you hate Earth. Once again, Henry Ruschmann is a dick.

## ONE LAST THING

If you live with your chick, and you're a slob who never cleans, have an excuse ready for when she comes home and asks, "What the hell happened in here?" Just lie and say that you wanted to do something nice for her for a change. And then watch her cry tears of joy.

## CLEANUP QUIZ

This is a crucial chapter, so if you get even *one* of these answers wrong, *read it again! No exceptions!*

**1. Poor planning and lousy time management have left you in the position of having time only to clean but not shower. Your chick will be arriving momentarily, and you reek of the scents of a strange woman. When your chick arrives and attempts to hug you, you should:**

(a) just take the hit, hug her, and pray to God she doesn't smell anything.

(b) leave the front door unlocked. When your chick enters, be standing a great distance from her with a towel wrapped around your waist. Exclaim, "Can't wait to get my hands on you! I'm gross and sweaty, though, so let me shower real quick." Then flee to the bathroom and do so.

(c) tell your chick that you were at the mall, trying out new perfumes you're thinking of buying her for her birthday.

(d) hope that a last-minute lie (for instance, "I'm sick!") will prevent you from having to engage in a hug.

**2. When you meet the mark, she's covered in glitter. She looks like a goddamn pixie. You should:**

(a) fuck her and deal with the glitter worries later.

(b) try to bang her in the shower, in the hopes that the water will dispose of any glitter evidence.

(c) end the encounter immediately, even if it means slamming the door in her face.

(d) lecture her on how glitter is bad for the environment, and, as a committed member of Greenpeace, ask her to go home, wash it off, and return afterward.

## 3. When the mark leaves jewelry, you:

(a) dispose of it immediately by any means necessary.

(b) keep it and give it to your chick as a gift.

(c) hang on to it until the opportunity arises to sell it for a small profit.

(d) keep it and use it as an excuse to see her again.

## 4. Which of the following of the mark's disposables are okay to leave in the trash can?

(a) tampon wrapper.

(b) candy bar wrapper.

(c) wrapper from a DVD she bought when you took her shopping.

(d) none of the above. Empty the fucking trash cans.

## 5. You're making love to your chick, and she feels something uncomfortable and hairy in the bed under her lower back. She reaches down and produces a hair extension, then screams, "Where the fuck did this come from?" You:

(a) say "How should I know? Stop it. You're acting crazy and killing the mood."

(b) run out of the house and hide.

(c) say "That's been there for years. You never noticed it before?"

(d) realize that you have absolutely fucked up and now need to follow one of the last-resort techniques provided in the troubleshooting section of this book.

**Answer key:** (1) b, (2) c, (3) a, (4) d, (5) d.

# Chapter 7

# The Art of Deceit

*Lying Like a Woman*

Even more important than the cleanup is the cover-up. But before we get to the intricacies of creative truth telling, let's talk about honesty.

This is a book about cheating, so it should be clear that we think a little bit of lying can be a positive thing. But there's a difference between fibbing outright and avoiding a cold, hard truth. There are plenty of instances outside of a cheat scenario when fudging the truth is not only constructive but necessary. Lying doesn't automatically make you a bad person. In fact, being brutally honest with everyone all the time doesn't necessarily lead to righteousness. It usually leads to everybody hating your guts. For example:

## Your Wife

She says to you, "I think I need a boob job. Thoughts?"

Don't jump up and down, clapping your hands, screaming, "Sweet! It's tit time! Finally!" We know that's what you're thinking, but keep that shit to yourself unless you want her to leave. Then you'll be wifeless and titless.

Instead, say, "Your breasts are beautiful and perfectly splendid the way they are. But if a boob job will make you happy, then go ahead, dear." Boom! Lie = new tits!

## Your Boss

He asks you, "Are you happy working here?"

You're thinking, "Fuck no. Happy? The only reason I haven't slammed my stapler into my eyes and then jumped out the window is because I'm afraid I might survive and not be covered by these shit benefits."

But then you say, "Of course I'm happy. See you at the picnic!" because you can barely afford to eat as it is. And the picnic has free food.

## Your Friends

An old buddy confides in you, "The wife and I keep trying to have a kid, but it's just not working." You search for the right thing to say, but all that's going through your head is, "That's just your dick letting you know what a cataclysmic fucking mistake you're attempting to make." Instead you buy him a beer and let him know that something as precious as human life takes lots of time and love to create. Then you tell him that, if needed, you'll help him find an adoption agency.

## Yourself

You are the one person you should never lie to. You spend enough time bullshitting other people. You're the home team. Never fuck with the home team. Being brutally honest with yourself strengthens your morale, mentality, well-being, and self-esteem. These things need to be intact, especially during a cheat.

Now, when dealing with the other woman, the way you separate or combine truth and deception depends on the person, the situation, and your preferred approach. Here are the options:

## The Sociopath's Approach: 100 Percent Fib

Though it may seem incredibly simple, this is actually the most complicated approach to cheating. Obviously, it's easy to lie if you're traveling and dealing with a mark you'll never, ever see again. But as far as a day-to-day operation is concerned, lies are like spinning plates: it takes a tremendous amount of movement, concentration, and poise to keep them from crashing down around you.

Also, lies feed on other lies—and they're extremely hungry. It's insanely easy to inadvertently immerse yourself in such a pool of deceit that even *you* can't distinguish fact from fiction. And not only do you have to remember your own lies, but also your friends and the people around you have to remember them too. Think about this: when your side piece thinks that she's your main squeeze, you suddenly have to incorporate her into several areas of your life—work functions, social gatherings, dinners with friends, and so on. If you don't, she's going to smell a rat. And once that happens, no more puss-puss. This is counterproductive. Lying to her is the least of your worries. Soon you'll be feeding bullshit constantly to your wife/girlfriend, then to your kids, then to yourself. That's the kicker.

Once you start believing your own nonsense, you start living in an alternate reality that doesn't really exist. That's what mental patients, sociopaths, and serial killers do. Do you really want to be like them? We didn't think so. You should probably choose another route.

## The Minimalist's Approach: Black-Belt Honesty

Some guys just want to bang with no emotional connection. Dump and run. This minimalist strategy is for when you are sick of having to keep track of a hundred lies, so you admit straight up that you have a girl and yet want to bang someone else. You score less often with this technique than with other approaches, but these guys are the safest long-term cheaters in the game.

It can be risky to pretend that you care about a cheat. In this day and age, where you can log on to the Internet and view your apartment building from outer space, it probably wouldn't be too hard for a scorned lover to find out where you live and ruin your life. When you pretend to care, like it or not, you've begun a relationship. And a side relationship is a land mine waiting to be stepped on. To avoid this, you need to get to the black-belt level of honesty, where you are 100 percent honest with your cheats. In other words, from day one, you tell them exactly what the deal is. This might sound crazy, but you'd be surprised what 100 percent honesty will do in one of the most dishonest moments of your life. It opens the door to getting away scot-free.

Every woman you meet simply wants to know what she's getting into. That's it. No more, no less. Sometimes the worst thing you can do to a cheat is to give her hope. Instead you tell her from the outset that you are in a committed relationship, and that, for the most part, you are happy, but every once in a while you want something different.

Now everything is on the table. She's either going to go for it or not. If she taps out, it becomes that Robert DeNiro moment in the movie *Heat*: you have to be willing to walk away. And don't be upset if this happens. You just avoided getting involved with a cheat who could go psycho on you if she found out what you should have told her from the beginning. If she hangs in there, you move up to the next level: that is, once you're done philosophizing about relationships versus the natural laws of attraction.

When the natural laws of attraction win out, she'll ask you something to the effect of "So . . . is this just going to be a physical thing?" At which point you say, "Yes." This is the lying equivalent to "runner's high." Amazing conversations can happen after this, provided that she doesn't bail. This level of honesty with your filth opens the door to talking about sex, and exactly what kind of sex you want.

It also allows your cheat to do the same. A lot of women are not satisfied in that area of their lives. That's because many females don't want to scare away potential husbands by telling them what they really want in bed. But in you, she's met a man who's told her that he has no interest in pursuing anything beyond the physical, and the worry of being judged is out the window. This opens the door for you to fuck the shit out of her without having to worry about her showing up on your front porch.

The last obstacle is a judgment call. Ideally, you just want to bang someone once and never call again. But if for some reason you want to go back for seconds or thirds, you must space out your visits. This will avoid anyone catching feelings. Don't get greedy. Swing by once every six to eight weeks, and you should be fine.

Have fun!

## The Romantic's Approach: Mixing the Two

You might think that honesty and lying mix about as well as water and oil, but that's wrong. They can mix as deliciously as water and Kool-Aid. In fact, many cheaters masterfully weave honesty and lying together like fine silk. In most cases, guys want to be honest with the girl they're cheating *with* and lie to the girl they're cheating *on*. That's the standard approach to infidelity. But if you can blend the opposites of truthfulness and deception, you will have an amazing power at your disposal. After all, it's the technique that made the devil so goddamn cunning.

This is the method used by the Romantic Cheater. For some guys, cheating is not all about the sex. It's about everything that takes place *before* the sex: the romance, the first kiss, and the spewing of mushy bullshit that they saw in a movie. These guys are looking to re-create the passion they lost in their own relationship without losing half their shit. The Romantic may have higher numbers, but with that comes a much higher risk of getting caught.

First off, just like in the Minimalist approach, tell the cheat that you're in a relationship. Honesty right out of the gate will make the gal feel special: "This guy is in love with another woman, but he likes me so much he can't help himself."

Now, enter the lie. She doesn't have to know how serious your relationship is. Play it down. Be very vague or refer to it as being "in dire straits" or "damaged." You've given the mark just enough truthful information to draw out her own fantasy about where the affair is headed. She'll have anywhere from a glimmer to a wellspring of hope that things will eventually work out in her favor: "This guy is stuck with another woman, but he likes me so much he'll probably leave her."

So far, so good. You are on the side of doing right by this girl—even though you are *so* fucking wrong. By the way, she's no angel either. All that shit she says to you, "You're in a relationship. We shouldn't be doing this. I want to, but I can't," isn't really meant for you. When she starts talking like that, she's arguing morality with herself out loud. Because in the end, she's just like you: a dirt ball. It's just that sometimes a girl needs an excuse to be dirty. You have to give it to her.

Time to weave: "I like being with you." "Talking to you is so easy." "I haven't felt this way in a long time." Translation: "I want to put my penis in your mouth and then fuck you in the backseat of my Chevy and then go home to the woman I love."

After you feed her the silk, it's time for the first kiss. Sex will come later. And we're not talking about a week or a month from now. We're talking about a matter of minutes. You need to get her as worked up as you are. Once you two are making out, instinct is going to tell you to start grabbing tits and ass. *Don't do it.* You'll just be setting her up to say, "No. Stop." Once the mark says that, it's back to square one. Just kiss her. Passionately. Do this for at least fifteen to twenty minutes, like you're back in high school. Throw in a few intense hugs too. And make sure to breathe softly in her ear—the kind of breathing that says, "Where have you been all my life?"

Now bring the whole session to a close with a slow, light graze of her vagina. If she reacts pleasurably—like you actually just inserted yourself—it's showtime. She's probably juicier than a peach that sat in the sun all day. The bang is upon you. It's going to happen. Right now. Not to mention that all is beautiful, and she's feeling nothing short of being swept away: "This guy is going to leave that other woman. He's in love with me."

Now you've banged her—so cut her off. How? Easy. Being somewhat honest at the beginning of this whole thing gave you the perfect escape route. "My girl found out, and she's pissed."

This, of course, is a partial lie. Your girl doesn't know shit. But if she did, she definitely *would* be pissed. Once again, our two friends, truth and deception, are working together. Because of this, the mark can't flip out. You told her from the get-go about your situation. And even if she does get angry, she's got no ground to stand on. All of her lashing out and screaming is just her way of saying, "I just realized that I too am a hunk of shit!" Allow her to do this. She's purging. Don't defend yourself; *agree* with everything she says regarding you being a scumbag. It'll be your good deed for the day. If you drop the bomb on her over the phone—*which you should*; you don't need to be part of a big, dramatic scene in public—she'll probably end up hanging up on you.

She'll achieve two things by doing this: closure and regaining some dignity. She stood up to you and walked away on her own terms. Good for her. And good for you. You pulled it off, you fucking rat!

## Lying Like a Woman

Brett Favre, Tiger Woods, that Nazi-looking biker guy, Kelsey Grammer, Kobe Bryant, Eliot Spitzer, John Edwards—kind of makes you think that only guys screw around, doesn't it?

But how many times have you or a friend banged some girl who had a boyfriend, or was engaged or even married? That's the genius of women. It's the way they wrap the package. They dress it up. They put a bow on it. They make it smell good.

There's a line from the movie *Titanic*: "A woman's heart is a deep ocean of secrets." Doesn't that sound beautiful and mysterious? That same statement about a man would read, "Guys are lying sacks of shit."

The reason why guys suck at lying is because it doesn't come naturally to us. The whole basis of being a man is to not be a bitch and instead just say what's on your mind. There is nothing in the male handbook that talks about being coy. You're supposed to be John fuckin' Wayne.

If some guy gives you shit, you punch him in the face. If

you go to prison, you take it over and eventually break out while simultaneously causing the warden to commit suicide. Be a fucking man.

Of course, most men fail to reach that level of manhood. Most live with being browbeat all day and don't truly speak their minds until they climb into their car and scream at their windshield for the entire ride home.

But nevertheless, lying never quite feels right to a man. Whenever you're being less than honest, in the back of your mind you're always thinking, "I'm acting like a bitch." That voice wears on you and can eventually get you busted.

Why is it that women are such good liars? Who knows? But we do have a theory, and a way to learn from them.

Guys are mainly about physical strength and tend to try to force things. For a female, the option of using physical force works for the first eight to ten years of her life, when little boys and girls are roughly the same size. But after that, she has to start using her brain to get what she wants. It's all about manipulation and finesse to get her way.

Ask the average man to manipulate or finesse a situation, and he'll fall flat on his face 80 percent of the time. Most guys wouldn't even have an idea how to begin. The lone few who would be great at it would consist mainly of pimps, politicians, and addicts.

But a woman is like a duck in water in any situation she needs to manipulate. Most women are so good, they'll not only get you to do what they want, but they'll also actually have you think that it was your idea.

Here's a situation that took place between Bill and his girl one night:

I remember driving home with this broad, and I mentioned that I was going to get a milkshake at a local diner.

She freaked out and was like, "Oh my God. They make the best milkshakes. But God, they are so big. Why do they make them so big?"

She kept insisting that the milkshakes were too big. My first thought was, "The milkshakes aren't big. They're the same size as any other milkshake." But after the fourth or fifth time she insisted that the milkshakes were too big, I began to think, "Yeah, how am I going to finish it?"

Fortunately, I'm a dick, so I was able to get out from under her spell long enough to realize that the milkshakes were the normal size.

So I said, "What are you talking about? The milkshakes are regular sized." Then she sort of looked away, and it hit me like a bolt of lightning.

"You want half my milkshake, don't you? You're on a diet, you want something sweet, but you don't want to annoy me by asking for half of my shake. Wait a minute! Did you just try to mind-fuck me into believing that I can't finish a fucking milkshake on my own?"

A cute, mischievous smile spread across her face. Even more fascinating was the fact that I felt I had earned a new level of respect from her, because I wasn't dumb enough to fall for her little game.

That's why women never get caught cheating. They are constantly practicing how to become better liars! Who would lie about a milkshake?

Stop putting your woman up on a pedestal. We're sure

she is an angel—but never forget that when you are in a relationship with a female, you have a fucking tiger by the tail. Women are so good at lying that when they get caught cheating, they can actually get out of it by blaming you.

"I cheated because you weren't paying attention to me."

"You worked too much."

"You never said the things I needed to hear."

As a man, try coming up with the male equivalent to those ridiculous statements:

"I cheated because you didn't cook dinner enough, and I needed to be with someone who had my back."

"You didn't blow me for, like, four months, and I felt as though you'd stopped caring."

"You put on a few pounds, and I needed to feel like I could still be with someone who was in shape."

See? It doesn't work for us. And it shouldn't work for them, but it does! We guarantee that women cheat almost as much as men. But it is usually kept secret, because most guys are not going to admit that their girl cheated on them.

If your woman strays, it's a blow to the male ego. The man feels like he messed up. And he can't turn to his male friends for support, because most of them are already trying to figure out how they are going to fuck his girlfriend.

So the male usually suffers in silence and, even worse, stays with the female, trying to heal his ego by attempting to fuck the little whore out of her.

This is one of those shitty hands that life deals us. Whether it's genetics, cultural nurturing, or just plain dumb luck, there's no changing it. The same way that some people can eat lasagna every day and never get fat, be born into millions of dollars, grow up in the south of France, or have the ability to run laps around a cheetah without ever getting winded, women possess an inexplicable, unfair advantage when it comes to deceit and manipulation. That's not an insult to their gender. We're jealous. Really goddamn jealous. But as much as we'd like to stomp our feet and scream, "Why not us?!" we won't. The constructive move here is to recognize our weaknesses and avoid them. To be the eight-millionth book to quote from Sun Tzu's *The Art of War,* "All warfare is based on deception," so learn your form of deception, its strengths and weaknesses, and fight the good fight.

# TRUE CHEAT

**Account by Bill Dawes, comedian, Broadway actor**
**Outcome:** *fail*

I was in a long-distance relationship with this girl in LA. I live in New York. It was a great relationship, but we had a little bit of a policy—spoken; unspoken, maybe—that I could dip my wick and be physical as long as I wore protection. It was a little unclear, and I guess I took advantage of that lack of clarity.

I did a TV talk show in New York and ended up flirting with the host: this forty-five-year-old woman. I gave her my number. So one night she texts me when my girlfriend is out of town: "You wanna fuck?" I instantly got hard and zipped on down to her building, where she had a penthouse. We had sex—without protection. The reason I didn't wear a condom was that this woman was in the process of having a surrogate carry her baby, so she had to undergo blood tests and have her eggs harvested every two weeks. She kept telling me about how safe she was. In my head, that justified my not wearing a condom for those four or five times we slept together. Eventually I felt guilty, so I ended the affair. And we didn't talk for a while. My girlfriend suspected something was up, but I never told her. I just figured I could swallow the guilt myself.

After a couple of months passed, the woman contacted me again to hang out. That's when I finally told her that I had a girlfriend. Well, she started talking about me on her radio show—anonymously at first. Somehow, though, my actual name got outed.

My Twitter blew up, and I started getting emails from her fans and all this crazy stuff. So I wrote on Twitter, "Wow, I got a bunny boiler situation on my hands." That set this woman off a little bit more, and things got even more heated between us. But even with all of this happening, I really thought that was the end of it.

A month later, my girlfriend calls me and says bluntly, "Tell me about this woman named _____. What happened?" I was like, "Oh my God." I didn't know what to tell her; I didn't know how she'd found out or what she knew. She never goes on Twitter, and even if she had, nothing on my profile mentioned any of this. All the negative tweets about me were on other people's pages. So I was confused. How did my girlfriend find out?

It turns out that this woman, while I was having an affair with her, was detailing all of this stuff on her radio show. Some anonymous person emailed my girlfriend a link to the transcripts. She read them, and they were too detailed to deny. So I was pretty much pinched, and I ended up confessing everything that I was comfortable confessing. I did admit the no-condom thing, which was a huge deal breaker for my girlfriend. Needless to say, we aren't dating anymore. We tried to work through it, but it didn't pan out.

## The Fuckup

Jesus Christ almighty. We wouldn't have seen this pinch coming if it was swinging its fists and screaming two feet in front of our faces. Talk about "Hell hath no fury."

The radio host talked about their affair, albeit anonymously, on her show. In detail. And when poor Bill's real name finally got mentioned, she made no effort to give the guy some cover. We understand that she was pissed off and all, but don't kick a man when he's down! Still, that wasn't the worst of it. The truly damaging thing in this situation was that some rotten weasel bastard anonymously sent Bill's girlfriend a link to the radio show transcripts. Sometimes you can't cover all the bases. String theory doesn't apply to cheating. There's no way to determine or predict the behavior and outcome of all the involved parties, actions, and factors.

The butterfly effect is always in full swing, meaning that any one of your actions can generate much greater reactions somewhere down the line.

In this case, Dawes pops his willy into a nice lady. Then, a few months later, his girlfriend gets an incriminating email from someone who wasn't even part of the banging.

What the fuck?

Anyway, the lesson to be learned here is "Know what you're getting into." Before you pop it in, take time to determine the worst-case scenario if things go south. For example, if the mark has a fucking radio show, be aware that your name just might turn up on it. And even if one of her henchmen doesn't take the time to send your girlfriend transcripts of what was said about you on the air, you still need to be aware: *it's a fucking radio show!* Your girlfriend, or one of her friends, has a decent goddamn chance of stumbling onto it by accident.

Even though Bill eventually got caught, he dodged an initial major bullet with the Twitter thing. His name and details of his escapades were all over that shit. Sure, if his girl went to his profile, she wouldn't have seen any of it. But all she had to do was run a search of his handle, and it would've been game over. We can't say this enough: keep your dirty laundry off Twitter and Facebook! The only safe site is Myspace, because nobody fucking uses it.

In the end, Bill's lady left him. Maybe it was because of the no-condom thing. Maybe it was because he misinterpreted their "open" relationship. Maybe it was because an entire radio audience was privy to details about how he likes to conduct his boning. We think it's simply because he got busted in the messiest and ugliest way possible. That sort of thing leaves a terrible taste in a lady's mouth—one that all the Listerine in the world can't wash out. And it happened because he messed around with the wrong piece of side puss. Guys, you need to be wary of a gal who texts you "You wanna fuck?" and then lets you bust off in her raw, without your even buying her a cup of coffee first.

We get it. That all sounds awesome. But a woman like that probably isn't the most stable individual, and therefore, when she gets upset, she's capable of doing any crazy shit under the sun.

So the next time you get a text, email, or phone call that gives you instant wood, proceed with caution. You may end up on the airwaves.

**FAIL**

# Chapter 8

# Tools of the Trade

*Using Technology for Hookup Success*

Technology evolves dramatically, but desires do not. Men are the same horny bastards they've been since the Stone Age, but today just about every person on the planet is walking around clutching a cell phone with video, picture, texting, recording, and email functions in addition to the mundane capability of placing calls. We've all become mini J. Edgar Hoovers.

Consequently, no one is safe anymore. Movie stars, rock stars, politicians, and average Joes are dropping like flies from the added surveillance. Everyone is getting caught—sometimes even in the act itself. Back in the good old days, it was so much harder to get caught stepping out. People got busted for things like having lipstick on their collar, someone calling the house and hanging up, or a love letter found while cleaning out the garage.

The public didn't know about JFK hooking up with Marilyn Monroe until long after their deaths. Now, if Barack Obama tagged Snooki, how long do you think it would take for the world to find out? Within twenty-four hours, we would not only know all about it, but could also watch grainy cell phone video footage on www.obamabangssnooki.com.

Technology is an amazing thing. It's almost angelic, allowing you to talk to women from all walks of life—women that you would never have been in contact with before. But it's also the devil. Technology can turn your life into one of those old-school horror movies where the mad scientist gets mauled to death by his own creation. Your cell phone and laptop can be your best friends, but in a second, they can become that dude who can't keep his mouth shut. With each form of advanced communication come risk and reward. However, if you follow these simple rules, you should be able to navigate the rough seas of today's technology.

## Social Networks

### Facebook

First things first: never check the "Keep Me Logged In" button on *any* social network site. If you are always logged in, anybody can go on your computer and immediately access your account and all the damning information in it. Yeah, it's a pain in the ass to have to type your password every time you log in, but taking the extra couple of seconds could save your marriage.

Always keep a low profile on Facebook. If you haven't

done so already, make sure that your account is not open to the public or searchable on the web. If your wife or girlfriend inquires about your new James Bond status, just give her some line about the "oversharing" of today's society and how you've rethought the whole social network thing and want your life to be more private. Feel free to rub your chin meaningfully while you pontificate.

In the meantime, use the site to troll for some ass! Upon meeting a mark, let her know that you rarely check your account and that the best way to get in touch with you is on your cell phone. (And yes, later on we have some rules about using your phone too.)

Once you get a dialogue going, your mark might send you a friend request. Don't accept your cheat as a friend because it will pop up on your real girl's feed. If your mark sends you a request, don't accept it or deny it. Just leave it. Now you don't have to worry about it showing up on your girlfriend's page, and your mark can't give you shit for turning her down. Just tell her that you'll accept it, knowing that you never will.

One difficulty you might run into is that you've been on Facebook for years and have taken a picture of every moment of your life since 2008. Hence, it's not going to make sense to your cheat that you don't want to talk on Facebook.

"Ohmigod, like, you have five thousand friends and, like, two hundred photos! We *met* on Facebook. Like, what is your deal?"

If this is the case, you have to adopt an attitude that you're "over Facebook." Talk about Facebook the way the Hollywood crowd talks about a formerly hot club that is now "so last year." Tell her you rarely check your account anymore. Once again, get her over to the cell phone. Once she's on your cell phone, you only have to worry about *one* person catching you rather than the entire free world.

Eventually your cheat will figure out that you're acting shady and something must be up. But if you have any skills whatsoever, you've already banged her and aren't returning her calls.

After hooking up with your cheat, watch your Facebook profile like a goddamn hawk. It's a good idea to change your password too, just in case your real girl is suspicious. If your profile is on private and you haven't accepted your cheat as a friend, there shouldn't be any way for her to leave some psycho comment on your wall like, "Did I do something wrong? WTF?!!! And to think I thought you were a nice guy. *Fuck you!!!!*"

But even though your mark isn't a friend, she can still *send you a message.* Once again, check your account frequently to delete anything damning. Unless you cheated with an absolute loon, things should die down rather quickly.

But always be aware of the "Hell hath no fury . . ." factor of a recently used-up mark. Never underestimate a woman. Your cheat could somehow befriend someone on your list of Facebook friends and have her leave a comment or God knows what else. No cheat is ever 100 percent fail-safe.

## Twitter

In a lot of ways, Twitter is even worse. It has all the dangers of Facebook distilled down to their purest form. No pictures, status updates, or friend requests, just the damaging statement right out in the open for everyone to read. Don't ever give out your Twitter info to a cheat. There is no real safe way to go about it. You could try direct-messaging her, but eventually she's probably going to send you a tweet, at which point you're going to get caught. If we can find out from Rob Lowe's Twitter account that Peyton Manning is going to retire before ESPN does, you think you have a shot when @blewyoulastnight sends you a tweet? Too much risk with too little reward. Stay away from Twitter.

And while we're on the subject of social networks, be sure to avoid dating sites as well. Those things are meant for relationships, and that's not what you're seeking.

## Cell Phones

When you're messing around on your chick, you must have your phone on Helen Keller mode. Shut off every ringer, buzzer, and bell. If you're fucking around and you don't have your phone on silent mode, your ringtone might as well be a recording of Rip Taylor singing "I'm *cheating*!" But as dangerous as phones are, they are also a tremendous plus.

With the capabilities of today's cell phones, you could literally set up some side ass while locked in the trunk of your kidnapper's car. The ability to call any woman, at any time, anywhere, is the upside to cell phones. I challenge you to call one woman in Miami, another in Atlanta, and a third in Los Angeles, all within ten minutes, and not feel as badass as Captain Kirk. The problem you will run into is having females calling your phone while your real girlfriend is around. There are two possible solutions to this problem:

Solution 1: Program your cheat in your phone under a guy's name or even have it show up as your place of work.

Either way, you can blow off these calls in front of your girl without looking suspicious. You might even get some props for not wanting to talk to your buddy "Mark" because you are too busy spending quality time with your girl.

Solution 2: Put your phone on silent mode as much as possible and especially late at night. No one calls late unless he needs to be bailed out of jail or she wants to fuck. If your phone rings during Leno's monologue, you are going to get the third degree from your woman. Someone really should come up with a "cheater" mode for cell phones. Until they do, keep your phone on silent and your eyes on your phone. Which brings us to the other dangerous aspect of owning a cell phone.

## Texting

Text messages are a great way to set up a rendezvous with a cheat, provided that you delete them as you go. Texts can be like a bread-crumb trail that leads right to the guilty, dumb look on your face.

The upside to texting is that you don't have to answer or whisper into your phone at odd hours. You can actually do it right next to your girlfriend, so long as she trusts you. A great time to text and set up a cheat is while you're watching a sporting event on TV. Your girl will think you're texting your "bro" about the game, when you're really arranging for some ass. Another advantage of texting is that your phone doesn't ring or need to be answered when you get a text. If it does, go into the personal preferences and turn off any sort of buzzing or ringing that notifies you of a new text.

The downside to texting comes when you fuck up and forget to delete an incriminating one, or even worse, leave your phone unattended for your girl to go through. Both scenarios are game-set-match moments. So if you prefer the texting route, you have to watch your phone like it's an infant in a room full of lead paint. Which brings us to . . .

## Emails

Emails are a lot like texts except that they don't vibrate when you receive one. At least, not on your laptop. But they shouldn't vibrate on your phone either, because you read the cell phone manifesto, right?

Emails are a little harder to hide than text messages. There are a few extra steps to watch out for. You need to make sure that you eliminate all received and sent bullshit emails to and from your cheat, so as not to give your snoopy girlfriend or wife a reason to be suspicious. Keep emails direct and to the point; it's all about figuring out when and where to meet your cheat. Don't get involved in any sexual conversations. That opens the door to receive emails with subject lines like "I want to suck your dick!!! ROFLMFAO!!" And while we're at it . . .

## No Pictures

When it comes to pictures, you have to treat yourself like you're a mob boss. No photos, ever. You don't want any proof that you were anywhere near another woman. When you take a picture with a mark, she can upload it to her Facebook page for the world to see before the night is even over. Even worse, if she's one of your FB friends, the picture that she just posted of the two of you will show up immediately on your wall too.

No pictures. Ever.

## Passwords

Don't ever give your woman or anyone else your password, even if you've deleted damning emails. There's always a chance that a mark could have sent another message since the last time you had a chance to check your in-box.

# TRUE CHEAT

**Account by Bill Burr, comedian, actor, coauthor of this book**

**Outcome:** *fail*

Once upon a time in a small, overpriced studio apartment far, far away, I was in a relationship, and things were going pretty good. And by "pretty good," I mean that I knew I wasn't going to marry her, but I was too much of a pussy to break up with her.

So I was going through the motions and trying to figure out when was a good time to have "the talk." In the meantime, I ended up meeting this gorgeous woman at a club. (You like how I'm acting as if I didn't facilitate this entire situation? I do that a lot.) We started talking, and I could tell that she was into me, and I knew that I was definitely into her. If I didn't have a girlfriend, this would have been one of the greatest nights of my life.

For me, the worst part about fucking around is the "having a girlfriend" part. It really messes up your ability to just go with the moment and bring some new girl back to your place. I had this weird thing where I didn't mind fucking around on the side, I just hated all the sneaking about. (I know, I know, I'm a fucked-up piece of shit who is trying to add an air of nobility to my dirtbag decisions. Well, fuck you. It's what I do.)

This new girl I met asked me if I had a girlfriend, and for some strange reason, I decided to tell her the truth. It was a watershed moment during the formative years of my illustrious cheating career. Up until then, whenever I was asked the "girlfriend" question, I always said no and then began sweating like a perp on *The First 48*.

But for some reason, I didn't lie this time. It wasn't even a conscious decision. Her question was hanging in the air, and I felt this calm come over me. It was one of the rare moments in my life when I actually acknowledged an emotion and then acted on it. "You know what? Fuck it." I looked her right in the eye and said, "Yes. Yes I do."

Her next logical question was, "Then why are you talking to me?"

I figured I was already halfway down the honesty trail, so there was no reason to turn back now.

I said, "Because every once in a while you see a woman and you just have to talk to her. It doesn't happen often, but when it does, it's beyond your control. [Dramatic pause.] You're one of those girls." Yes, it was corny as hell, but I meant it, and she believed every word of it. Why wouldn't she? I was telling her the truth. Not to mention that I looked like Ralph Malph, so I think her defenses were down.

The conversation continued, and I answered all her questions honestly. It was unbelievable. The more I told her the truth, the more she seemed to want to fuck me. Being a typical moron guy, I thought, "I'm doing this every time! This is great! What could go wrong?" About ten minutes later, we were kissing a little bit at the bar.

A quick aside here: years earlier, I received a couple of great tips from older pieces of shit who were trying to help out the young piece of shit that I was becoming. Here's one:

"Never give them a chance to second-guess what they are about to do." Basically, once the romance of the one-night stand begins, do not press Pause at any moment. If I had a dollar for every time I missed out on getting laid because I had to stop to buy some condoms, I'd have enough money to buy three hot dogs and a Coke at Yankee Stadium or the entire Milwaukee Brewers franchise (take your pick).

"Just keep 'em laughing. Keep being affectionate. Whatever you gotta do. That's what it's all about." It's in those moments when you hit Pause that women start to think about what they are about to do—and in my case, what they are about to do with a man who doesn't possess any pigment.

Back to the story: After we left the bar, I suggested that we go back to her place. She told me that she lived in Jersey and had roommates. "Fuck . . ." is what my brain thought. But my dick quickly appended an "it" to the end of that sentence, and next thing you know, I was taking her back to my place.

My girlfriend at the time did not have keys to my apartment, but she used to drop by regularly. It was not unusual for her to come over late at night after she was done working.

It was an unbelievably reckless decision. I had no out. No backup plan. No story. All I had was a roll of the dice that, hopefully, my girlfriend wouldn't show up.

My cheat seemed oddly turned on by the fact that I was risking my entire relationship for a fling with her, which was causing more and more blood to leave my upper body and head due south. Back at my place, we did the deed. It was a classic one-night stand: over in well under twenty minutes. I was psyched, and she seemed pretty happy too—at least, that's what my ego told me. However, in the moments after we were done, I noticed this woman start to take on a different mood. Or, as a black man in the early 1970s would have put it, "The bitch was acting funky."

Something was up. She went from this cute, sophisticated woman to a watery-eyed fidget who seemed to be experiencing some sort of manic episode. I tried to keep the paranoid thoughts at bay, telling myself, "You were totally honest with her. She knows you have a girlfriend, so she obviously knows she has to vacate the premises immediately."

But as much as I tried to remain calm, I couldn't shake the fact that this woman was clearly acting strange. She had an odd smile on her face, and, for the life of me, I couldn't figure out what she was thinking. The energy hanging in the room told me not to leave this female alone for even a moment. But I had to remove the prophylactic from my member. The same member that had basically convinced me to go into this one-night stand the same way this country went into Iraq. Anyway, being a gentleman, I decided to tidy up quickly in the bathroom. I swear to God, I didn't leave this woman alone for more than eight seconds!

When I came back, not only was she still lying in bed, but she was kind of lying all over the fucking bed! She had no sense of urgency. And she was completely ignoring my "Shufflin' off to Buffalo" vibe.

"Why is she acting like this?" I thought to myself. "We had an adult conversation. She knows I have a girlfriend. Why won't she hurry up?"

I started to get mad. But, thankfully, that's when I remembered this essential advice for cheaters: don't ever yell at a crazy woman. Stay calm and waltz that nut job right out of your life.

Acting on the advice of my elders, I slowly walked over to the bed and put out my hand, as if I were the most romantic man on the planet. As I did, I saw one of her eyebrows twitch. Her face relaxed, and she took my hand, rose up out of the bed, and began to s-l-o-w-l-y put on her clothes.

Meanwhile, I was dressed in about three seconds. Then I just stood there waiting . . . and waiting . . .

An awkward silence filled the room, and in a desperate attempt to break the tension, I asked her if she wanted something to drink. The second I asked, I knew it was a mistake. But I had to keep the "chill" façade going so this maniac didn't make a scene.

She, of course, said, "Yes. I'd love some water."

For the next eleven excruciating minutes, I watched her slowly sip this glass of water. Fucking lipstick on the rim of the glass, the whole nine yards. I sipped my own glass of water and leaned against the counter, trying to act as if I didn't have a care in the world.

I was convinced she could hear my heart pounding.

This time bomb finally finished her water and headed to the door. But there was one last hurdle.

"Aren't you going to walk me out?"

"Sure." I walked her down five long flights, convinced that at any second my girlfriend was going to suddenly appear in front of us like Jack Ruby, and I was going to take one right in the gut. When I finally got her outside, she asked me some shit about where she could catch the train back to Jersey. I quickly hailed her a cab, gave her twenty dollars and an awkward semi-affectionate hug, and she was out of my life. Waltz completed.

I then raced back upstairs to begin the cleanup. First I washed her lipstick off the glass, and then I attacked the bedroom. When I got to the bed and pulled back the comforter, I looked down and saw one hair extension, placed ever so carefully underneath the sheet. My stomach fell.

First of all, who knew that white girls wore extensions?

And secondly, I'd fuckin' told her I was in a relationship.

Why would she do that to me?

It took finding the extension for me to finally figure out that this girl simply wanted to get me caught. She was a classic psycho. She was oddly turned on by the situation initially and then did the classic Glenn Close/*Fatal Attraction* postintercourse flipout.

Out of pure dumb luck, my girlfriend didn't show up that night, and I was able to clean up the crime scene. But for two weeks afterward, I worried that every time I walked out of my apartment with my real girlfriend, the psycho chick was going to be there, waiting to get back her hair extension.

## The Fuckup

That our hero didn't get caught does not matter. There was no skill involved in this maneuver. This story is basically the cheating equivalent to when a basketball fan is pulled out of the crowd and actually hits the half-court shot—only to win a key that *might* start a new Dodge Neon.

Bill should have walked away the second his cheat said she lived in Jersey and had roommates. Instead he got greedy and took a chance at messing up his entire life because of some psycho he met at a bar. This is the exact kind of decision that professional athletes, politicians, and celebrities make right before they get caught. And it's the exact kind of situation that this book is trying to get you, esteemed reader, to avoid.

On paper, no man would ever go forward with the above game plan. But most men get overruled by their dicks, and that's why it's so important to have your dick in check.

# Chapter 9

# Paying for It

Strip Clubs, Massages, and Women of the Night

If you're having a hard time meeting the "other woman"—or just want to play it safe—you can consult a professional whose job is to rid your dick of its demons. Cheating doesn't always have to consist of an affair. There is always one thing that can get you around a legitimate personal interaction: money. At the strip club, at the massage parlor, on the street, or at the whorehouse, pay attention to these tips for getting the most bang for your buck. But remember, we're comedians, not lawyers—so don't come whining back to us if our advice lands you in the county lock-up for a night.

## Strip Clubs

Most strip clubs are just really expensive bars with some T&A on display. Not that this is a bad thing: seeing some girl's stink wrinkle for a few bucks while chatting it up with some pals over a brew is what heaven should be.

Strip clubs are fantastic if you don't mind staring at naked women and going home with blue balls—or wearing sweatpants with no underwear and getting several lap dances in the hopes of reaching completion in the saddest way possible. However, you'd better hope that the stripper is cool with that, because if she's not, you run the risk of some big, angry bouncer splitting your head open. If you're looking to really get your cheat on, it might not be the place for you. For the time and money you're spending, there are much more efficient methods available.

Now, you may not consider visiting a strip club "cheating" because you're not really having sex with any of these girls. At most, you're going to walk away with sticky underwear and piss in eighteen different directions the next time you go to the bathroom. But would you like it if some hot guy with a huge piece was grinding it all over your wife's cheeks while you were at home watching a *Star Wars* marathon on Spike TV? Of course not.

Be honest: if one of these fine ladies wanted to leave with you or take you in the parking lot and do some nasty shit to your pee-pee, you wouldn't stop her. But that's not going to happen unless you're famous or really good-looking.

Most guys just want to see naked women dance on a stage while enjoying a beverage and making small talk with a friend. You're a hunk of shit all day in your cube at work, stuck in traffic, in line at a bank or a pharmacy, but when you walk into a strip club, you are a king, with naked women dancing around you at all times. They look you in the eyes and fawn over you like you are the most important man in the room.

This is all bullshit and part of the game, of course. But fuck that "reality" bullshit. "Reality" is not why you go to a strip club. You go because you get to have some hot eighteen-year-old girl sit on your lap and pretend to be interested in what you do and what you think—and at any point, you can bring her into a dark back room and have her take off her clothes and rub her privates all over you for twenty goddamn bucks.

The next day, you are back to work in that cubicle, standing in that line, waiting in that traffic. But it's all a little easier to take, and you don't have to worry about shit growing on your cock, getting arrested, or having some chick show up at your door telling your wife you got her pregnant.

## Not All Strip Clubs Are the Same

There are many different kinds of strip clubs, both in terms of the quality of the personnel and the limits to what they'll do. The standard club has some hot girls slowly peeling off their clothes while dancing to some cheesy song and occasionally swinging on a pole, but that's not always the case. Some strip clubs are topless only. Others have girls who show you where babies come out. And there are some joints that will let you touch the girls and the girls touch you. Of course, everything comes at a price.

As far as quality and class of show, you have your high-end strip clubs, your low-end strip clubs, and your downright freak shows. The difference between high-end and low-end strip clubs is the difference between Ruth's Chris Steakhouse and McDonald's. Both places are good, and you will be full as fuck when you're done, but the differences in price and quality are huge. It just depends on your mood. The high-end strip clubs usually have top-notch tits and ass showing their goods onstage. Most of them are large venues, have tons of girls working at any given time, and serve food. That's right: you can eat and have a hard-on at the same time. Some places even have sushi bars. Insert fish/pussy joke here.

When we say "low-end" strip clubs, we don't mean shit-holes to avoid at all costs. There's a slight difference between low-end and shit-hole strip clubs. A low-end club will have some worn-out-looking dancers, but you don't have to worry about getting stabbed. Here's a good rule to follow: if the club is connected to a truck stop, keep driving. Again, it's like McDonald's. Sometimes there is nothing like a Big Mac and a large Mickey D's fries. But it's not the fanciest place you've ever eaten, and the people who go there are not the most sophisticated. So if you're hungry to see some snatch that's not your girl's and you don't want to blow a whole paycheck to do it, these low-end joints are the way to go.

Then there is the freak-show strip club. You can tell these clubs have been around for years, and they are usually in more rural towns in the middle of nowhere. The building, by day, probably looks like it's scheduled to be demolished. But by night, the neon lights come on, the trucks and shitty cars pull into the dirt parking lot, and the fun begins.

The girls at these places . . . well . . . to put it simply, you might see a girl who resembles your aunt dancing onstage at any given time. But don't let the lack of bombshells stop you. These places can be more fun than any other strip club. For one thing, you are going to be more at ease because the strippers are chicks who you could probably get a date with in real life, and that adds to the illusion. Secondly, the girls have to do more than just dance to get a crowd to throw dollars at their average bodies. The outfits, the routines, and the extent to which they will go sexually far exceed those of the hot girls from a fancier joint. If you play your cards right, you've got a chance of getting a BJ in the lap-dance room.

No matter what type of strip club you patronize, keep the following things in mind to make your experience even more enjoyable.

## Choose the Right Time to Go

Most guys think that the best time to hit a strip club is after eight o'clock at night. Believe it or not, sometimes going in the afternoon gets you a little better service and a little more attention from the girls. But you have to know that you'll be dealing with the B team during the earlier hours. The girls are not going to be the best the club has to offer; it saves the A-team girls for the prime-time Friday and Saturday night shifts.

If you love baseball—I mean really love the sport—it would be like seeing a minor league game instead of the Boston Red Sox versus the Yankees. Are you going to have a good time? Yes. But will you be focused on the game as much? Probably not.

Now, going when the B team is on the field does have its advantages. For one, it's not going to be as crowded as it would be during prime-time hours. In addition, the daytime girls are more desperate for money. Not that they're going to blow you in the VIP room for twenty bucks, but they will be a lot nicer to an average guy such as yourself. The fewer guys there are for them to choose from, and the less hot the dancers, the bigger the bang for your buck. So if you don't have a few hundred dollars to throw down the toilet on a Friday night, we suggest going to a strip club during off-peak hours. But if the excitement of a packed club eyeballing the A team as it does its thing is what gets you off, then by all means go for it.

## Be Clean

Most strip clubs are lit in a way that makes everyone kind of good-looking—or at least it hides people's flaws. It's not so much for you as it is for the girls onstage. But you have to be careful of the dreaded black lights that most strip clubs have all over the fucking place. It highlights everything: dandruff, shirt stains, lint, and embarrassing dog or cat hair. You don't want to sit there wondering why no girl is coming over to you and discover it's because you're glowing like a UFO as the black light emphasizes what a fucking slob you are. Avoid this situation and take a second to give yourself the once-over before you leave the house. Make sure that your shirt doesn't have any stains, maybe shampoo your hair with some Selsun Blue, and for God's sake, use a lint brush if you own a furry pet. When going to a strip club, you need to be at the top of your confidence game to really enjoy your time.

## Don't Use an In-House ATM

Using an ATM at a strip club is as bad as . . . well, using an ATM at a strip club. Those bastards charge you whatever they want in fees, and it will leave a trail of where you have been on your bank statement. Stop at a bank ATM before you go to the club.

Once you're inside, order your first drink and hand the waitress two twenty-dollar bills: one for the drink and another for singles. The dollar bills are going to be your "set-up money," which we explain in the "Be Patient" section below.

### Use the Little Straw

Strip clubs put a little straw in your drink. Use it. Drinks at a strip club are very small and filled with ice, to get you to spend more money on overpriced alcohol. The straw will prevent you from sucking down your drink in one gulp and having to spend all the cash you brought for snapper on booze instead. Remember that you're there for the pussy, not the drinks.

### Adjust Your Junk

Before you enter the private room for a lap dance, make sure your junk is adjusted so that it can achieve its full potential. Reach down and get that shit over to one side when you sit down so that it's not uncomfortable when it starts to fill up. You won't be the only one to enjoy it. It makes the woman feel good too.

### Know They Are Acting

You have to accept that these girls want nothing to do with you. Even if they say they really like you and want to do dirty things to you, they are lying. Well, not lying, exactly, but acting the part that you are paying them to play. It's their job to make you feel good, so go with it. At the end of the day, it's a business transaction—all part of the game to get you to spend money. If you ever believe that the affection you're renting has an ounce of validity to it, you're going to end up back at that fucking ATM.

### Be Patient and Wait for Your Fetish

Treat your set-up money—that nice little pile of dollar bills in your pocket—like chips in a Texas hold 'em tournament. Don't go "all in" on the first piece of ass to walk out on that stage. The girls work in a rotation, and you should see the whole lineup before you go investing your hard-earned dollars. Now, you don't want to be rude to the girl onstage either. If you're sitting there watching and not tipping, she will go back and tell the other girls what a cheap fuck you are, and they will avoid you like you have genital warts. So throw out a little cash to every dancer onstage, but be patient. You want to wait until you see the girl who best suits your mood. And when you do, let it be known by giving her more bills than you gave the others. Then she'll know that you like her and, most likely, will come over to you when she is done dancing and say hello.

### Clean Yourself Up Before You Go Home

You might think that just because you didn't bang a chick, you are in the clear and your girl won't find out. Wrong! You need to take the same precautions that you would if you had just popped a chick in the parking lot of Chili's. Strippers have all kinds of smells and body glitter and shit to make them sexy to the clientele—evidence that needs to be disposed of if you don't want to get caught. And let's not forget the gallon of precum drenching your underwear. Before you get home, you need to find a bathroom and wash up a little. Check your clothes for glitter or stray hairs. When you get home, take off your underwear, roll it up in a ball, and stash it at the bottom of the hamper.

Or better yet, fool around with your wife a little. You don't have to go all out and bang her. Just do enough that it could explain the jizz stains on your underwear if she questions you the next time she does laundry.

## The Happy Ending Hot Spot: Asian Massage Parlors

There are places you can walk into in America and pay anywhere from forty to one hundred dollars to have some semi-good-looking Asian lady give you a great massage and then make you cum all over your belly.

And get this: they clean it up for you and give you a mint on your way out. Now, if that doesn't sound terrific, we don't know what does.

Massage parlors are perfect for getting what you need while managing to feel somewhat respectable. First of all, it's as anonymous as it gets. No one's going to see you. And if you do bump into an old buddy in the lobby, he's as guilty as you are, so he'll keep his mouth shut. Secondly, you're actually getting a massage, if you go to the right place. Sometimes your "massage therapist" will even wear a white lab coat, which gives the whole experience a "clinical," not "dirty," vibe. All of these elements make the hand/blow/fuck job at the end seem like the natural evolution of the massage.

There are two kinds of massage parlors. The high-end male spa resembles a sports club of sorts. It is a storefront stand-alone location that offers many different amenities and services. There are private lockers available to secure your belongings and valuables. There is a sauna and/or a steam room, and possibly a reception area where you're given a robe, and sometimes slippers, for your visit.

The more common version, however, is your basic no-frills Asian massage parlor. They too will have a front desk, but the massage room will be bare-bones, with just a table and a coatrack or place for your belongings. We think it's always better to go Asian. Broken English, coupled with the ladies' inclination to giggle, makes the discovery of your boner and the negotiation that follows quite charming and whimsical.

Don't confuse these places with whorehouses or mistake the women for prostitutes. Yes, some of them will suck and fuck you. For Christ's sake, they will stick things in your rump if you pay them enough. But that's not what we're advocating here. Not to say those options aren't fun, because they are. But whorehouses can be creepy and dangerous for the same reasons that certain strip clubs can be: a shady clientele/management/environment. Hey, even though we approve of them, there's a reason they're illegal.

Once you've located a possible venue via the Internet, phonebook, or word of mouth, find out its hours of operation. Most legit massage places don't stay open after 10:00 at night. So if the lights are still on at 12:22 a.m., chances are someone is getting jerked off in there.

Second, if it offers a table shower or body wash, you're good to go. No regular massage place is going to scrub your balls and ass as an extra.

Third, don't be afraid to walk the fuck out if you don't like what you see. Just walk the fuck out. If the place smells like old fish, get the fuck out. If the girl they give you has a German shepherd mole with a three-inch hair growing out of it, ask for another one, and if they say no, walk the fuck out. If there are too many people waiting for a massage, leave.

Don't stay because of your low self-esteem or because your dick is too hard. Just take a breath and leave. There is probably another place right around the corner that suits your dirty needs. You want to be relaxed when you're in there.

## The Buzzer System

Since some illegitimate activities go down in these massage parlors, security is important. For example, some places have a buzzer entry system.

Don't let this freak you out.

This is a good thing. Although there is a camera mounted somewhere looking at you when you're trying to get in, it means that the cops can't just waltz in unannounced. The buzzer-camera system is in place to weed out both cops and crazies, so don't look too nervous or suspicious at the front door, or they won't buzz you in. If it's your first time, go during the day just before or after lunch. It won't be that busy, so you will get a little more personal attention and feel more at ease. Depending on where you are in the world, the system may be different, so just relax and go with the flow.

## Cash Is King

Most massage parlors take all major credit cards. If you're single and are just banging a few girls who have no chance of ever seeing your bank statement, go ahead and whip out that bank card of yours. But if not, use cash. You don't want a trail leading your wife or girlfriend back to your oasis of joy. Even if it comes up on the bill as a Chinese restaurant, your woman is going to want to know why you ate a hundred dollars' worth of Chinese food at twelve thirty in the morning and whom you ate it with. Now, unless you're Dom DeLuise in the movie *Fatso,* your excuse will not fly. You can explain a cash withdrawal way more easily than a specific charge on your credit or debit card statement. You can just say that you got stuck picking up the tab at a cash-only restaurant for all your buddies at work, and then proceed to call them all drunken, cheap assholes.

Don't be afraid to throw your friends under the bus to save your relationship. They would do the same thing in your position. Just don't forget to fill them in on the story in case your wife brings it up at the company picnic.

## Less Is More

After you go once, the next time, bring only the exact amount of money, in cash, that you will need to drop your nut and find your way home. That way, you can't get into too much trouble. Sometimes they might offer you a little more for a little more. If you don't have it, you don't even have to think about it as an option. After all, this is an illegal transaction, and these places are kinda sketchy, so it's always better to be safe than sorry.

Before you go, check the massage parlor's prices either on the Internet or, if it doesn't have a website, by calling the business directly. Once you know the cost of your massage, put that exact amount in one pocket. Then calculate your tip money. (Yes, you have to tip, and I'm not talking the 15 percent you throw down at the end of an okay Indian meal.)

After a happy ending, you have to tip at least $40. Anything less, and the next time you go there, none of the girls will want to take you because you're a cheapskate, and your massage will be rushed.

Tip well. She is jerking you off, for Christ's sake.

A good rule of thumb is to take the price of the massage and bring double that amount with you. For example, if the massage costs $60, bring $120. You're not going to use the full $60 for a tip; you will tip $40 or $45. But you always want just a little extra in your pocket after you're done. You may be too relaxed to get on the subway and want to take a cab home. You will probably be hungry or thirsty and want to stop and grab something. If you have that extra $20 in your pocket, you're all set. If not, you will have to go to the ATM again, and, like we said before, that is a no-no. You don't want to leave bread crumbs for your chick to find. This isn't "Hansel and Gretel"; you *want* to get lost in these woods.

## Undress for Success

Hang or fold your clothes in a neat and orderly fashion and position them with the item of greatest importance closest to you. Put one sock in each shoe. This way, if something goes down and you need to get the fuck out of there, you're not scrambling to collect your clothes and can get dressed in a hurry.

Do not leave any valuables out or in view. Your wallet should be in the pocket of your pants. If you have a watch or another valuable item that you want to remove, it should be placed inside a pants pocket as well.

Don't put anything on the floor except your shoes. Besides aiding you in making a quick escape if necessary, you don't want any of your clothes on the floor, where they can pick up roaches or bedbugs.

Leave on your wedding ring. The novice might be tempted to remove it, but I assure you, it makes everyone more comfortable when it's clear that you're married. You're not the first husband to grace that table, and you won't be the last.

### Go Balls Out

Take off your underwear and be fully naked when you lie on the padded table. That way, they know you mean business. If you're wearing your underwear when the masseuse comes into the room, she might think you don't know what kind of place you're in and just give you a standard massage. Massage parlors always have you lie on your stomach first, so make sure that your junk is adjusted comfortably. Your dick should be in a good spot to fill up and get soft over and over again because, for the next forty-five minutes, that's exactly what's going to happen. Your cock will be her barometer to know what turns you on and what doesn't. When she is rubbing the back of your knee and your dick goes soft, she knows to go back up to your ass crack and inner thigh. Just make sure to position yourself in a way that you don't bend your dick too much and injure it, because a bruised cock is even more difficult to explain to your girl than a fishy credit card charge.

## Be Yourself—and That Means Not a Cop

Stay calm and collected from the moment you step through the front door. All massage parlors have a front desk, and the lady who runs the place will be sitting there. She will usually make the call to decide which girl you get, so be nice to her.

Don't be afraid to smile. She will probably ask you if you have ever been there before. This is a common "cop test." If you say yes, and she doesn't remember you, she might tell the girl to give you just a regular massage. Of course, if you say no, she might wonder why it's your first time and assume you're a cop. And that too means you get nothing.

The best way to answer her question is to say something along the lines of "No, I've never been here. I usually go to another place near my house."

Now she knows you're not a cop, and you know what you're there for. She doesn't think you're a newbie to this operation, just a newbie at that location.

Your masseuse will probably also ask you some questions once you're ready to go. It's a good thing to slip in what you do for a living as soon as possible. Remember, if she thinks you could be a cop, she will just give you a regular massage, which will frustrate you tremendously. There is nothing more aggravating than expecting to cum and winding up with blue balls. Sometimes they will take the initiative and ask you what you do. They're not trying to warm up to you. They want to hear you say you're not a cop. This is more of a common courtesy between you and the masseuse. If you assure her that you're not a cop, she can relax a little bit. It lets her know you're a part of the club—like the Freemasons' secret handshake. It's a creep code of sorts. Now, a real cop *is* allowed to lie at this point. However, he *cannot* allow the girl to touch his junk. Also, by following the nudity rule above, you will be further assisting your case, since according to a cop buddy of ours, it's illegal for cops to take out their penises on duty. So if the masseuse walks in and sees your bare ass spread out on the table, she knows you're a creep who wants to make cumsies.

### The Wrap-Up

Most places will take a nice hot towel and wipe you down like a prized racehorse when you're finished. If they don't, ask them to. You need to get all those foreign oils and powders off your body. You don't want to go home smelling like some cheap body oil your girlfriend or wife doesn't own. You think drug dogs have great sniffers? Well, women can smell ten times better than man's best friend when it comes to catching you cheating.

We all have a scent. And your girl could pick that smell out of a smell lineup. So get the aroma of evil off of you before you go home.

You're at your most vulnerable when entering and leaving the rub and tug. You want to go out like you went in: quick and easy, like you leave your own apartment. You don't think about leaving your place; you just leave. You know where the doorknob is and how many steps there are to the sidewalk. You want a fluid transition from one place to the other.

If you bump into someone you know, don't say anything. In most cases, the person won't even ask what the fuck you're doing coming out of that place. He probably doesn't even know what kind of place it is, but if he does ask, lie. How the fuck does he know if you're telling the truth? End the conversation as soon as possible and get home. Your mission is complete. If you did everything right, you should feel relaxed and calm, like you just had a private yoga session with the Dalai Lama. In summary, always ask yourself what Keyser Söze would do.

Your deviant act will leave not a single trace. Just like that—poof!—it's over.

## Women of the Night

These are a last resort. If you can't find any other way to get laid, and you need some action, get a hooker. Now is actually the best time in history to fuck a hooker. Getting a hooker before the Internet was frightening. You'd have to drive your car around some shitty neighborhood for hours, pulling up to random women, hoping they were "working gals." But that wasn't the worst of it. Once you got her in the car, you had to make sure she wasn't a cop. Or a man. Then you had to negotiate the money and services. And your work still wasn't done. Last but not least, you had to figure out a safe place to go to get your rocks off. Now, with the Internet, you can visit a website, pick your perversion, and choose your price range. We don't want to name them. We're not ratting out anybody. But if you're curious, ask a couple of your dirtbag friends or do a little Internet research. We're sure you'll find them.

Online brothels have extensive listings, information, and photographs, all for your shopping convenience. But be aware: most of the time, what you see in a picture isn't what you get. So, before the lady arrives, you have to temper your expectations. Or you'll have to figure out a polite way to return it— and by "it," we mean "her."

Escorts, lot lizards, brothels, whorehouses, streetwalkers, prostitutes. To the novice, these might all seem to be the same thing. To the expert, they are all very different ways to pay to get your rocks off. We will go through all of them and give you the information you need to get through any of these filthy experiences unscathed. All of these choices we have described run a certain risk of legal ramifications, but sometimes they are the only option for the real deviant in you. Sometimes the convenience and the ability to get exactly what you want sexually are worth the risk.

For instance, you might like a finger in your butt while you cum. Now, you can ask your pretty little wife or girlfriend to do that to your awful balloon knot. But what if she says no? Then you just feel like a creep. Not to mention what she will be thinking in her head about the husband she thought she knew.

And even worse, what if she says yes? Do you really want the woman you love, the mother of your child, putting her fingers in there? Every time she is feeding your kid, you will know where those fingers have been. This is not the case if you're married to or are dating someone who is just as freaky as you in the sack. But in most cases, you partner up with the girl who doesn't need double penetration every time you have sex.

Sometimes, paying for sex is as simple as filling the emptiness in your life. Women go shopping and become hoarders; they max out their credit cards and get fat; they have a baby. When a guy gets lonely or depressed, he bangs. A new pair of shoes just won't cut it. He needs to conquer something. Two thousand years ago, men could just go start a war and kill some shit. We could go into the jungle and hunt a wild boar. Those days are long gone. We have been deballed. We go to work every day, we have to say thank you and please and hold the door for some dickhead who doesn't even say thank you in return. And we can't smash him in the head and make him say it; we have to just take it.

Then we get home, have some low-carb meal our wife made for us because we are getting too fat, and we watch some mediocre TV show and commercials where guys are being emasculated by strong women. And then we get into a fight with our girl because we pulled her hair too hard while she was giving us a so-so blow job, and she was offended because we asked her to put a finger in our bum. Now we're just sitting there with a hard-on trying to forget this day ever happened, because we have to do it all over again tomorrow.

Having a pro do what you tell her to do, for a price, is not so bad compared to what we really want to do: kill people. A hooker pulls you back from the edge. And let's not forget the hunt. Prostitutes are not all the same; you have to find just what you're looking for. Sometimes that perfect sexual encounter is hidden on a random street corner or website, and you have to hunt it down like a deer in the woods. You might be looking for a twenty-dollar blow job because you can't afford a high-end escort; you have to hunt that down. There are some guys who like to be tied up and have nails hammered through their ball sac. Just because a girl sells her pussy for money doesn't mean she is a nutcase with a tool belt; you have to hunt that down. You have to know where your prey is, be prepared, and most of all, be patient. Like Jeremiah Johnson waiting for an elk to show his head through the tree line.

Whatever your reason for paying to have sex with a stranger, we understand. And we will help you.

Or you could do the decent thing and go to a therapist to work out all your fucked-up issues. But that's not what this book is about. This book is about not getting caught when you give in to your nasty desires to cheat on your girl. If becoming a better person is really what you want, they have a book for that too.

It's called the Bible, and it's much harder to understand.

### Brothels

You may think that a whorehouse and a brothel are the same thing, but they're not. A brothel is usually a more respectable place. And by "respectable," we mean that you're going to have to drop a mortgage payment to bust a nut.

Now, if you have disposable income or have been saving your pennies to play out your wildest fantasies, go for it. We couldn't see paying a thou to cheat on our girl. But who the fuck are we to tell you how to spend your money? It's not something you would do every week, like a rub and tug or a plain old streetwalker. It's more of a once-in-a-lifetime thing.

Everybody has to have goals, and this can be one of them.

There are around thirty legal brothels operating in Nevada at the moment. The majority of them are in the northern part of the state, near Reno and Carson City. Prostitution was also legal in Rhode Island up until 2009, when its party pooper governor Donald Carcieri put an end to it. We pray every day that he gets caught up in a sex scandal. What an asshole! Thank God Nevada is still corrupt enough to allow a man to pay good money to have his creepiest fantasies come true. That's the good thing about a legal brothel: the sky's the limit. Since you're paying so much, and you don't have to worry about the cops busting the place, you can do anything you want. Yes, anything!

Here is the sex menu from one of the most famous brothels out there: the Moonlight Bunny Ranch. (Can you believe that? They have a sex menu. It's like walking into an IHOP and ordering pancakes, except that it's pussy. Now, if they opened a place where you could get pancakes *and* pussy, I would move to Nevada.)

- Girlfriend experience
- Massage (give or get)
- Hand-relief party
- Vibrator show
- Bachelor parties
- Orgies
- Dungeon
- Blow job
- VIP rooms
- Champagne party
- Pamper party
- Love at the *Y*
- Half and half
- Bunny style
- Viagra party
- 69 party
- Full French
- Around the world
- Tantric sex
- Asian wet room

- Swinger parties
- Sybian experience
- Dinner dates
- Neapolitan
- Whipped cream party
- Two-girls party
- Overnight stays

- Outdoor and indoor Jacuzzi fun
- Fetish and fantasy
- Couples and single ladies
- Three-girls party
- Food, fun (*9½ Weeks*)
- Porn-star experience

We know what you're thinking: What the fuck is bunny style? We have no idea. But you can get it at the Bunny Ranch if you have the cash.

Another thing that makes a brothel cool is the atmosphere. You can walk in and not feel like a creep. Everybody knows what you're there for.

Most places have a full bar where you can hang out and get your drink on before you go in and do "the do." Some even have Internet access, so you can conduct a little business while you're waiting to bang. But what you are really paying for is a worry-free time. That's the reason you drove way out into the desert in the first place. If they had a legal brothel right down the street from your house, you'd run the risk of bumping into someone you know while you're there. The last thing you want to hear is "How much for the anal beads?" and you look over and see your kid's third-grade teacher. The next parent-teacher conference would be very uncomfortable.

We do suggest turning off your cell phone's GPS. You don't want your girl using some fucking crazy find-a-phone app to locate exactly where you are in the world. You are supposed to be in Las Vegas on business, and your phone says you're in Carson City.

Another thing you can check off your worry list by going to a legal brothel: these girls are clean. Since these brothels are legal, the state is responsible for making sure the girls working there are not endangering the health of their customers. So a physician checks them on a weekly basis. That's right. You don't have to worry about bringing dick bugs back to your significant other because these girls have been checked by the state like a side of beef.

Although visiting a brothel, financially and geographically, is not practical for everyone, if you can be patient, save your pennies, and happen to be in Nevada, it's a great place to get your freak on and not get caught.

## Whorehouses

Unfortunately, whorehouses have been almost totally wiped out of existence because of the Internet. There is no need for a girl to work at a whorehouse when she can just make her one-bedroom apartment on the Lower East Side her own personal sex den. She doesn't have to worry about splitting her money with the house, competing with other girls, or going with a guy she really doesn't want to be with because she is the only girl available at the time. She can pick and choose what she wants to do and with whom she wants to do it just by putting an ad on a sex site.

Of the whorehouses that remain, most don't have that much variety. That wasn't the case ten or fifteen years ago, before the Internet. Back then, you could walk into any whorehouse and find girls of all nationalities: black, white, Spanish, Filipino, Asian. Now they are mostly Asian, which is not a bad thing, but there was nothing like walking into a whorehouse and seeing some hot blonde who kind of looked like a chick you wanted to fuck from high school but never did. For a small fee, you could bang the one that got away or never was yours to begin with.

Even though the majority of whorehouses today have Asian workers, we don't want you to confuse them with your basic rub and tugs. The girls in a whorehouse will do more to your junk than go up and down for fifteen seconds until you make a happy face. And they won't be wearing the typical white doctor's smock or street clothes, like in a massage parlor. They will be in something a little more provocative, such as an evening gown or a swimsuit, to let you know that they mean business. So if you walk in and it looks like you just crashed a pool party, you're in the right place.

First, let's talk about what a whorehouse is and why it's different from a brothel. For starters, a whorehouse is not legal. A whorehouse is a really low-scale, illegal brothel, and, for the most part, the girls who work there are just a few steps above being streetwalkers. As far as safe cheats go, this is still one of the safest when it comes to not getting caught. Even so, you have to be careful when using these establishments. Why? *Because they're illegal,* which means that the cops could conceivably bust in at any time and haul you out in handcuffs with nothing but your bush fat covering your Johnson.

Second, since they're illegal, the girls don't get examined by a doctor like they do in a brothel. This doesn't mean that you are going to catch anything. These girls are still probably fine and cleaner than some chick you meet at a bar in Jersey and wind up banging without a condom in the parking lot.

The girls working in a whorehouse are going to make you "wrap it up" even if they're giving you head, but there are still risks.

Most owners of illegal whorehouses are criminals. If you think Dolly Parton is going to come down the stairs singing a song like in *The Best Little Whorehouse in Texas,* you're crazy. In fact, you will probably never see the owners, because they're too busy taking care of their other illegal businesses. But this is a good thing. You will probably be greeted at the door by a mature older woman who will inform you of the cost to be with one of the girls. That's usually a flat fee just to get in the door. There are no menus in these places. Everything else is negotiated in the room with the girl you pick.

After you pay your initial "cover charge," you will be brought into a room or a hallway where the girls will be paraded by. You get to choose the one you want, and she takes you to her room. That's where the real negotiation starts. She will have her list of what she will do and for how much already in her head, but here's where personality matters. If you're a dick and treat the girl like a whore, she will try to wring all the money she can out of your rude ass. But if you're nice and sweet, she might cut you a break and give you a blow job for the price of a hand job.

So like Patrick Swayze said in *Road House,* be nice.

As we explained in the section on massage parlors, you should compartmentalize your money. You don't want to pull out a wad of cash when it's time to pay. You want them to think that what you paid was all the money you had. Let them think they beat your sorry, lonely ass for your last dollar. And if you come back, they will know what you usually spend and won't expect any more or any less. If you come in balling with a wad of cash your first time, they will expect that every time.

Also, not every girl has the same attitude and demeanor. Don't always go with the hottest girl. Instead, find one that you like on a personal level. If she says hello or gives you a quick smile or a wink, you've got a winner. A little personality goes a long way when you are in the room about to negotiate for sex. This isn't a buffet where you can just throw everything on your plate and taste test. This is pussy: you can't just spit it out if you don't like it and try something else. You're pretty much stuck with the girl you chose at that given time. So if a girl is smoking hot but looks at you like you're a hunk of shit, chances are she is going be a bitch and charge you for her dignity. Then again, maybe you get off on having a hot chick who thinks you're a hunk of shit fuck you because it's her job.

Either way, once you find the girl who does it for you, stay with her. Get her name and call before you go to make sure she is working. Done in the right way, a good whorehouse can be a great and safe way to cheat on your girl.

## Casino Whores

*Casino whores* is pretty much self-explanatory. Now, if we said one-dollar chimney whores, that would require an explanation. But if you find yourself at a casino bar at three o'clock in the morning playing video poker and you look over to see some hot chick smiling at you, she is probably a casino whore.

Regular girls don't hang out by themselves in Vegas at

three in the morning. The great thing about this form of prostitution is that you don't have to go anywhere; they are right there in your hotel waiting for you to find them. You just have to know what to look for and when to look for them.

The best thing about casino whores is their hours of operation; you can usually spot one only late at night when the party is winding down. This way, you can spend most of the night playing the odds trying to meet and hook up with a "regular" girl—the odds of which, at least in Vegas, are pretty good, since there are plenty of horny tarts looking for some dirty, casual sexual encounter. It's not like you're at a local bar in Indiana trying to get laid; it's fucking Vegas. But if you do find yourself alone late at night wandering around the casino floor, wasting your money on the Wheel of Fortune slot machine, all you have to do is look around, and you will see random sexy girls just hanging out by themselves, waiting to be put to work. They are usually casually playing a slot machine or some video poker by the bar.

But beware: they are hunting you too. They are looking for the easy mark, the injured deer, the baby elephant that got separated from the pack. These are not the high-end escorts Vegas is known for. They are usually at the lower end of the food chain. But if you're in a jam and need to dump your seed so that your vacation doesn't have an asterisk next to it, these girls will do just fine.

Now, you don't want to just walk up to the first girl who smiles at you and ask her if she is a hooker. That's like congratulating a girl on being pregnant when she might just be fat. Walk around and take notice of your surroundings. Play the game One of These Things Just Doesn't Belong Here. It may be a lone girl by the bar dressed for a night out on the town or a girl in some slutty outfit in the middle of a slot machine bank not really paying attention to what she is doing. When you see a girl by herself looking as lonely as you, sit down next to her, order a drink, and just say hi. If she turns her back or exits the situation, she is probably not in the game. But if she eagerly continues the conversation, you might just have a winner. Make sure you exchange your info (your name, what you do for a living). Don't be afraid to lie: she will understand.

Like any sex worker, she needs this information to make sure you're not a cop. And *you* need this information too. If you run into hotel security or someone you know—your pals, some girl you went to high school with—you need to know the girl's name and act like you're friends, so they don't know you're actually with a whore. Never forget that you are being watched by the eye in the sky. They might not have been watching you the whole time, but they sure as hell have been watching her. And now that you're with her, they are watching both of you. So be cool and play the game. You are not going to do any negotiating on the casino floor. In fact, she will probably let you think you are actually picking her up. Go with it.

Here is the hard part:

Ask her if she wants to have a drink up in your room, at which point she should say, "I would love to."

Not really that hard, was it?

Get up and start walking to the elevators. Have your key out and ready to go because there is always security by the elevators in a casino. Keep the conversation moving right along, and before you know it, you will be in your room about to get your sex on. The second you get into the room, place all your valuables in the safe. This includes your wallet, your watch, your money, and anything else you don't want stolen. You don't have to worry about offending her at this point; she is in the room and wants to make some money.

Here is where the negotiations will take place. She will probably bring it up, and if she doesn't, don't worry, she will when you're finished. But it's better to do the negotiating at the beginning, so you know what you're getting into. Think of it as participating in an auction for an antique car. You have to have your top price, and you can't go over that number no matter what. We don't care what she offers you. Don't get sucked into banging a girl for an extra hundred because she starts telling you how cute you are and how she really wants to have sex with you. At this point, you're just trying to get the evil out of you so that you can enjoy the rest of your vacation. A hand job or a blow job will do if it saves you a few bucks. Instead use that money to tip the poor maid who is going to have to pick up all of your crunchy towels piled in the corner of the room the next morning.

When you finally agree on a price, you're good to go. The casino whore might want her money up front, which is perfectly normal. Go over to the safe and take out exactly that amount—no more, no less. And get this: you can even pay them in chips! How cool is that? You can toss a girl a clay chip to suck you off, like you're in a Frank Sinatra movie.

When you are done, she will probably want to use your bathroom. If you did what we told you to do and put all your valuables in the safe, you have nothing to worry about. Other than that, don't let her out of your sight. Make sure you are wide awake at this point. We know you just busted a nut, and the natural response is to take a nap, but don't you fucking dare. You need to get her out of the room ASAP. This is when you turn all business. Thank her for a great time and walk her to the door. As soon as she leaves, lock that fucker, do a room check of all your shit, and make sure she didn't take or leave anything. Take a shower to get the stink off and order yourself some room service for a job well done.

## Streetwalkers

Yes, the streetwalker still lives. Thank God there are still some places where you can find the most electrifying hunt left for a man, next to hunting a rhinoceros.

The hunt is the aspect of the cheat that most people don't understand. They just think guys want to pay to bang some girl because they can't get laid any other way. Not true. Sometimes it's about the hunt. The sex act itself is the last thing we are thinking about. It's everything before the sex that gets our dicks hard: Getting the money. Driving to that fucked-up part of town and prowling the streets—sometimes for hours—looking for the perfect prey to approach and do our dealings. Negotiating a price. Letting a strange girl into our car, not knowing whether or not we're going to be arrested at any second. And, finally, finding the perfect spot to take out our piece and let her do her job.

A lot of the same rules apply when going with any of the safe cheats, but with a streetwalker, you must follow them religiously. The risk level is high, and you have the greatest chance of getting thrown in the clink for the night. We're not saying that if you get caught with a hooker you still can't talk your way out of it. But as with most things, it is better to avoid getting caught at all.

## THINGS YOU SHOULD KNOW IF
## YOU'RE GOING TO USE A STREETWALKER

First thing, no matter what, always wear a condom! In most cases, the streetwalker will have rubbers with her, and she'll make sure you put one on your gear. This is their job. As with any job, they have to come to work with the proper tools. It would be like a painter coming to paint your kitchen without his roller. If she doesn't have a condom, you might want to rethink going through with it. Where hookers are concerned, you always want to think about the worst-case scenario. And in this case, if you don't use a condom, that could mean AIDS, herpes, genital warts, and/or syphilis, to name a few. But getting any of those awful dick diseases isn't even the end of it. You have to take into account giving it to your girl when you go home: the woman of your dreams, the mother of your children, your high school sweetheart, etc. What the fuck did she do to you besides fail to turn you on anymore? She doesn't deserve that. So wrap it all the time, every time. No fucking excuses.

The second thing you have to be careful about is whom you pick up. Not only can she be a crazy, fucked-up crack addict, she can be a cop. Make sure you find out. A good way is to ask if you can grab a tit or if she will grab your junk. No undercover cop is going to let you squeeze her cans, never mind put her hand on your nuts. Now, let us be perfectly clear: if she *is* a cop, you can get arrested for asking her to do this. Again, it's the creep code we talked about in the massage section. But if she does cup your balls or let you molest her tits, she is definitely a genuine pro. So you can both relax and move on to more important matters. There is no surefire way to find out who you're dealing with until you ask. But that's part of the excitement, isn't it?

Lastly, set up a place to bring her ahead of time. Don't be driving around in your car with a prostitute, looking for a place to go. You think your wife can get impatient driving around the mall parking lot during the holidays, looking for a spot? These bitches will cut you. Most of the time, they will have their spots where they like to go to do the nasty, so it doesn't hurt to just ask them, "Hey, do you know of a place where you can suck my cock for twenty bucks?" Wouldn't that be the perfect first date with a square chick? But the line will work only if you're on a date with a hooker, my friends.

## Online Escorts

When people say the word *prostitute,* what usually comes to mind is a half-naked girl in fishnets and high heels hanging out on some seedy street corner, sashaying up to car windows and trying to negotiate her sexual skills for money. That's a pretty accurate visual. But with the invention of the Internet, this tried-and-true practice has become obsolete. No longer do working girls have to stake out their spot, worrying about the cops who bust them and the pimps who abuse them. Nowadays, finding a woman for paid sex is as easy as turning on your computer and searching for exactly what you want sexually. You might think that this would take the hunt aspect out of the equation, but a cyber hunt can be just as exhilarating. Whenever something dies, it is reborn into something new. And so we come to the online escort.

## WHAT IS THE DIFFERENCE BETWEEN AN ESCORT AND A STREETWALKER?

Basically, an escort is a hooker who works from home. The terminology you need to know for this is "out-call" versus "in-call." An out-call is when the girl will come to your place; an in-call is the opposite. We do not suggest using the out-call option, as this can get really dangerous. Most girls travel with a menacing bodyguard, and you could have all your money stolen, or even learn that the bodyguard carries a gun. If something goes wrong, you would rather have it go wrong at her place instead of yours.

Having so many options on the Internet makes finding exactly what you want somewhat harder. There are things you have to look out for with an escort. For one, when you are on the streets looking for a girl, what you see is what you get. Not so with the Internet. Most of the time, when you show up at her door, it's not going to be the girl from the online ad. So you have to be able to walk away. If you show up at the door and it's not the hot eighteen-year-old blonde you saw in the picture but a thirty-eight-year-old redhead with zits, just turn around and walk away. Or be willing to take the hit, because once you step in the door, you're not getting out without dropping some cash. Here are some things you need to know if you're going to choose the escort route:

1. You are going to pay way more for sexual acts with an escort than you would with your average streetwalker. There are deals to be had using an escort from the Internet, but you have to hunt them down like an old lady clipping coupons.

2. Make sure you use a reputable sex site to choose your girl. What makes a sex site reputable? Well, first of all, it should offer a lot of choices. For example, you should be able to select from a range of states and cities and a full menu of sexual experiences to find exactly what you are looking for in your price range.

3. When you call these places, make sure to use your cell phone and erase the numbers when you're done. If you find a girl you like, you can keep her number in your phone, but make sure you save it under a guy's name, like Bill DeRosa. And don't call a bunch of them in a row; spread them out a little. Call a friend in between so that if your girl does get a hold of your cell phone bill, it doesn't show a bunch of numbers with the same area code over and over.

4. Don't be afraid to ask questions when you call. They might hang up on you for sounding too suspicious, but fuck it. It's better than showing up and having some dude in drag kick your ass for wasting his time. Unless that's what you are looking for, in which case, go for it.

5. Know the terminology. If an ad contains the word *independent*, it doesn't mean the girl has a strong will and opinions. It means she works for herself and not an agency. Independent girls are usually cheaper because they don't have the overhead of paying a company to set up their dates. *Full figured* = "fat girl,"

*mature* = "old lady," and so on and so on. Learn these terms so you can find exactly what you are looking for.

One of the best things about using an escort is that it's discreet. This also makes it easier for the average girl to become an escort, because she doesn't have to walk the streets and deal with a pimp to get dates. The girl next door can sell her goods to pay her college tuition and student loans. A downside to this is that you might bump into her on the street with your girlfriend or wife. So don't go with an escort who lives in your building or even in the same part of town. The last thing you want to hear while you're walking your dogs with your chick is "Oh, how cute!! What kind of dogs are they?" And when you look up, it's the girl you paid a hundred and fifty dollars to give you head two nights ago.

Like all cheat options, the escort comes with its challenges. But if you are willing to do the work, you can overcome them all and get your sexual cheat on in a safe way.

## Lot Lizards

This section isn't for everyone. It's relative to who you are and what options you have available. Okay, it's mainly for truck drivers and creeps who hang out in truck stops. We're not saying that truck drivers are creeps. We fully understand that there are not a lot of sex options for a guy who has been driving for the last thirteen hours and has to stop in the middle of Texas to sleep in his truck. Thank God for the girls who provide service to the men who keep America moving! However, we *will* say that if you don't have a truck but hang out at truck stops for some pussy, that's a little creepy. If you're expecting to find quality, you're going to be thoroughly disappointed. Still, you need a little sun and a little rain to make a rainbow, so let's talk about the good stuff first.

The convenience of lot lizards is a plus. In most cases, you just have to park your truck, and they will come knocking. One by one, you can either oblige her or tell her to beat it. These girls will also advertise themselves on the CB radio, indicating where they will be and at what time. They will usually ask for a "donation"—that's code for how much it will cost you. Another great thing about these gals is that they're cheap and quick.

As for the biggest downside to these girls, most of them look like Uncle Fester with a wig. But remember, you're not paying regular prostitute prices here. We're talking fifteen bucks for in-the-truck sex; a little higher if you want to fuck around in a hotel room. We don't care who you are (or who they are): that's a bargain! And the risk of getting caught is low because you're doing it in your truck. It's not like cops are setting up sting operations at truck stops around the country. So if you are in need of a really quick fix and don't have the time or money to seek out the perfect piece of paid ass, a dirty old lot lizard might be just what the doctor ordered—along with that penicillin you're going to need.

## Online Pornography

If your girl finds out that you've been spanking it to BBWs or MILFs or TVSTs or some other creepy acronym, you'll probably be in some shit. So never, ever download any smut. There's no need to do it anymore—you can stream it all in your browser. And be sure to empty your cache. Again, *empty your cache*! This is a simple, untraceable step that takes two seconds, yet so many guys refuse to do it and end up getting their asses chewed out. And stick to the free sites: Tube8, PornHub.com, YouPorn, Cliti.com, etc. Pay sites will appear as a "legitimate" business on your credit card statement, but that can actually be worse. Sometimes it's easier to just admit "I bought porn" than to try to explain why there's a thirty-dollar charge to "US Consultants" on your Visa bill. We're firm believers in never confessing, but as far as cheating goes, porn is pretty passive. It's a good way to take the edge off, and it's more or less guilt free.

## Cheating? Seriously?

Yes, some women actually consider it cheating if their man watches porn on the Internet. Not too surprisingly, the authors of this fine manual do not agree with this sentiment. We'd define it as healthy, sometimes shameful or embarrassing, or even comical. You have to admit, there is a bit of silent film comedy when you've finished and you have to do that Charlie Chaplin shuffle into the bathroom with your pants down around your ankles.

But *cheating*? How in God's name is watching porn cheating?

Is it because you have an orgasm while looking at another woman? Is that what it is? Because if that's the case, we would argue that having to block out the undercarriage view of the male genitalia with accompanying taint whilst we're jerking off kind of cancels out leering at another woman via computer screen.

The computer screen is another area of major disagreement. How can you be guilty of cheating when you are watching something on a computer or TV screen? It isn't a real human connection. If a man sits down and watches *Scarface,* is he guilty of drug trafficking and mass murder? If you were to watch a History Channel documentary about D-Day, could you then claim to be an honorary war veteran and member of the Greatest Generation? Of course not! Then how is watching a porn clip an act of adultery?

It's a ridiculous argument, and until they come out with a full-body virtual sex suit with matching 3-D glasses, we don't believe that this argument would ever hold up in a court of law. But if the case were to be tried in a kangaroo court of finger-snapping daytime talk-show hosts, with a jury of soccer moms, we would advise you to try copping a plea.

In a logical world, Internet porn is not cheating. But we don't live in a logical world. And since a lot of men simply want to keep the peace at home and in their relationship, many of them routinely go along with this asinine antiporn argument, even though, secretly, they don't agree. This leads to sneaking around with a laptop and watching porn in the darkness of a walk-in closet. No studies have been conducted as of yet, but there is a rumor that watching porn this way ruins your eyesight and could lead to thigh cancer.

The truth of the matter is that watching porn actually helps a man to *not* cheat on his wife or girlfriend. Rather than banging some girl at work, a man simply finds a look-alike at a free online porn site and proceeds to rub one out. Where is the harm?

It's kind of like when you're on a diet, and you're craving sugar. Rather than eating a pint of ice cream, you eat a piece of fruit to get your fix. Both foods contain sugar. But one is clearly a shitty, less appealing substitute for the "real" thing. That's what porno is: the healthy choice to replace going out and cheating.

So for any man reading this whose woman won't let him watch pornography, here is what you should do if you get caught: explain to your chick that porno is the male equivalent to the romantic comedy. For the most part, no guy wants to watch a romantic comedy, and we don't understand why anyone else would either. A lot of women feel the same way about porno. They think it's horrific and that there is something wrong with you if you want to watch it. Well, we feel the same way about all those Hugh Grant movies that costar that actress with the squinty face.

When used correctly, pornography actually helps a man to remain faithful. The end result? Empty balls, clear head, and no "situation" at home or at work. There is no need to hide your cell phone, delete emails, or worry about STDs. It's a clean, healthy substitute. Porno helps a man to not cheat in much the same way that violent video games help men to not go postal at the company picnic.

Now that we've presented our argument about why pornography is a good thing, it's time to urge a little caution. Like everything in life, there is good and bad, yin and yang, zippity-do and fuckin' something else.

You have to be careful with porno. It's not like it used to be.

It used to be an *event* to go out and get some porn. You had to not only pick the right day, but also the right time of day. You had to put on some ratty Michael Moore baseball cap and avoid eye contact. You'd get into your car and drive to a *video store*. With any luck, it would be an overcast day, thus decreasing the likelihood of someone recognizing your car.

In small towns, you'd enter the establishment and walk past all the legitimate movies—like *Scent of a Woman, Interview with the Vampire,* and *Days of Thunder*—until you got to the back of the store. You'd glance around to see if the coast was clear, while never making eye contact with anyone, and then walk through those swinging saloon doors to get to the stuff you really wanted.

When checking out, you had to get over the fact that you felt that you were going to be judged. You had to face another human being, holding the VHS of filth that you wanted to indulge in. Sure, there were always creeps who didn't care, but for the most part, the dude behind the counter kept everyone in check. You could indulge only so much without feeling like a creep.

With online porn, however, you have complete freedom to look at as many clips as you want for as long as you want. And you are free to look at the sickest, most fucked-up shit you could possibly imagine. (Every regular porn viewer has that one clip he wishes he never saw.) All of this behavior will remain anonymous, never to be judged by your fellow man—unless you decide to run for president.

So it's up to you to keep yourself in check.

Too much of something is never a good thing. You have to monitor your online porn viewing and make sure you aren't disappearing down the rabbit hole. If you aren't careful, the next thing you know, the only thing that gets you off is *Anal Mascot Midget Fighters, Part 7*.

Here are three dangers to avoid in your online pornography viewing:

## 1. Porn Addiction

The World Wide Web contains many a slippery slope, all of which are beckoning you, waiting to desensitize your soul and put your penis in the position of being able to erect itself only at the sight of some really weird shit. In other words, watch out for what you jerk off to. Try to keep it within your general wheelhouse. You know, stuff that you think is hot yet normal.

The second you find yourself thinking, "I wonder what this fetish is all about?" you're in trouble. Eventually, secret fetishes manifest as suggestions for stuff that you and your girl should do on "special occasions." She's not going to appreciate the suggestion. For starters, she hasn't been watching all the porn you have been. She thinks you have a decent relationship. Also, guys with addictive personalities have to be particularly careful when it comes to Internet erotica. It will only put the taste of blood in their mouths and eventually lead them into several despicable sexual situations that will haunt their psyches like Vietnam flashbacks.

Free porn websites are kind of like ESPN. On paper, it's a great idea. Actually, it's a fucking dream come true. But then somewhere along the line, it becomes too much. Sports highlights used to air each night at the end of the local newscast for about five minutes. That's all you got. Sports fans used to pine for more sports programming. When ESPN came along, a twenty-four-hour all-sports network, it was heaven.

But next thing you knew, guys were missing important

deadlines at work because they were too busy watching fat fucks play Texas hold 'em poker.

Having twenty-four-hour access to pornography is kind of the same thing. You have to be aware of how much you are indulging and see to it that this great invention isn't consuming your life. If you feel you're watching too much, take a couple of days off, if not a week. Make sure you control it. Not the other way around.

## 2. Drifting Away from the Mother Ship

Think about the first porno you ever rubbed one out to. For most people, it was pretty tame. All you needed was to see two people having sex. Regardless of the position or the scenario, you were good to go. But over time, very subtly, you needed a little bit more. Or maybe your tastes became a little more specific. Or perhaps something that you initially found disgusting suddenly began to turn you on.

This is the type of thought process that you have to be aware of. If you aren't careful, you can slowly drift away from the PG-13 stuff that first turned you on and end up watching all kinds of horrific shit. Once again, this has never been proven in any official study, but it is our view that if you go too far, you lose touch with regular people and end up being that creepy guy in the trailer park who doesn't seem to have a job or own a pair of underwear.

If you feel you've drifted too far from the mainstream, try this: take a week or two off from watching porn, and when you come back, just watch striptease videos. Pretty bland stuff, compared to what's out there. Rub one out to these videos for about a week or so and then slowly upgrade to the

PG-13 porn that used to bore you a few weeks ago. Hopefully, it will be a little more exciting. If you find yourself slipping up again, just take another break.

It's kind of like when you booze too hard. You go on the wagon for a few weekends and get yourself in check. Treat porno the same way.

### 3. Becoming Lazy

Watching pornography is akin to eating at Arby's. It's not going to kill you, but you know it's not good for you. No intelligent human being sets out to eat fast food. It sneaks up on you. You're hungry, you're tired, you want instant gratification, so you choose the path of least resistance. Similarly, why go out tonight and spend a bunch of money trying to get laid when you can just stay at home and rub one out for free?

Economically, that plan makes sense. But as far as being a man and keeping your game tight, that's basically about as disciplined as Shaq's off-season workouts were. At the end of the day, you want to be having sex with hot women for real. You don't want all your conquests to be a computer screen, which is one of the dangers of watching too much porn. You'll empty your nuts, lose your drive, and the next time you get an opportunity to get some side action going, you'll be about as smooth as a mathlete at an eighth-grade dance.

# TRUE CHEAT

**Account by Noam Dworman, owner of New York City's Comedy Cellar and Olive Tree Cafe & Bar**

**Outcome:** *fail*

I had been caught cheating over and over again—movie stubs, condom wrappers, you name it—by the same woman and by other women. I was like the gang that couldn't shoot straight. Finally, I realized that the only way to get away with it was to ensure that nobody but you and the girl knew, and to go somewhere where no one would recognize you. Because I've been in that situation where you're out in public and someone recognizes you.

I was cheating on my current girlfriend, Juanita, with this other girl, and I decided to go to Washington, DC. I figured it was far enough away.

So I pick the other girl up in the middle of the night, we drive down to DC, and check into a hotel. It was fantastic.

The next morning, we wake up around ten or eleven o'clock. My phone's been ringing and ringing, but I don't want to answer it because I don't want anybody to know where I am. But finally, I answer it, and it's Ava, my father's wife.

She says frantically, "Oh, thank God! Where are you? We've been looking all over for you! We were so worried about you!"

I'm like, "What are you talking about?"

She goes, "Haven't you put on the TV?"

I say, "No. Why?"

So I turn on the TV. It was 9/11.

The Twin Towers have come down, everything is in a state of

panic, and I'm in DC. I'm like, "Oh, shit!" And I couldn't get back to New York. How am I gonna explain this? I tell Ava, "Don't worry. Everything's fine. We're in DC. We went away for the weekend." I didn't tell her anything more.

Meanwhile, Juanita's mother is also in a panic looking for her, and she comes running to the restaurant I own because she figures that's where we would be. She finally makes it there, and she finds Ava, who's the co-owner of the restaurant. Ava says, "Don't worry! They're in Washington, DC." And my girlfriend's mother says, "They're not in Washington. I saw Juanita this morning!" So then it all clicked, and Ava realized what was going on. I was busted.

It would be a few days before anyone could get back into Manhattan. They shut down everything. I remember wishing that it would just go on and on and on, so I wouldn't have to come back and face my girlfriend.

But she forgave me, and we got married. They always forgive you. But it's like 9/11: they never forget.

## The Fuckup

Wow. When the judicial forces of the known universe decide that your number is up, your number is up. Ain't no fightin' it.

Noam didn't really do anything wrong here. In fact, he pretty much did everything right. He learned from his previous mistakes, he made note of how and why he got popped in the past, he formulated an excellent strategy, and he brought his mark to a safe zone where he could bang away without consequence. Or so he thought. Karma had other plans.

Can you imagine?

If you can't, allow us to browbeat this into your head. You're off in another state, nobody knows your whereabouts, you're in a glorious and carefree mood, reaping the benefits of your flawlessly executed plan, and then the greatest tragedy in the history of the United States happens. Fuck. You were just supposed to get caught on that day. Plain and simple.

If you go through all that trouble and end up getting pinched by a terrorist attack, then you were doomed before you even left the house. No matter what Noam did, he was fucked. Even if he stayed home and didn't cheat, he would've gotten caught cheating. His girl would have been doing laundry and found a hair or bobby pin attached to one of his shirts or some shit like that.

The one slip-up Noam committed here was that he told his father's wife, when she called in a panic, that he wasn't alone. That's what burned him. When the phone rang, Noam should have excused himself from his cheat's presence to take the call and then explain to Ava that he was on a trip and flying solo. (This is why he needed to excuse himself. Even if the cheat knows that she's the cheat, she doesn't want to be made to *feel* like the cheat.)

Had Noam told Ava, "I'm in DC alone," she would have asked him why. Then Noam could have said, "I'll explain later." Then Ava would have said, "Please explain now." Then Noam could have said, "This is a time of crisis! Enough with the interrogation already!"

We realize that unless you're one of those sightseeing douche bags, it might be tough to justify a trip to the nation's capital by yourself. But shit, due to the attack, he was locked out of New York for days anyway, so he had plenty of time to think of *something*.

Upon his return, a simple "I needed to get away and reflect" probably would have sufficed. After all, Noam owns a bunch of bars and nightclubs, and successful businessmen do introspective shit like that sometimes.

But maybe Noam wasn't concerned with taking any extra precautions. Maybe he figured he did enough already. Maybe he thought that, in the wake of a terrible event like 9/11, his infidelity would be water under the bridge. Maybe, when Ava called, he assumed that his back was against the wall and it was blaze-of-glory time. Maybe he was feeling like Tony Montana at the end of *Scarface*. You know, he put up a hell of a fight, but now they've got him surrounded, and there's no way out. "I take all your fuckin' bullets!"

Or maybe he just knew his girl would forgive him.

Whatever it was, and despite its outcome, this journey was epic. *Epic*.

# Chapter 10

# Going Global
## Cheating Around the World

Going out of the country to cheat is a great option for the guy who *really* doesn't want to get caught. It also helps reduce the guilt factor substantially.

Depending on the time zone you're in, it's like you never even cheated at all. And you don't have to worry about seeing anyone you know or bumping into your wife or kids. Not only that, but outside the great old US of A and its puritan outlook, other countries don't view sex as a bad thing. In some places, like Rio de Janeiro, Brazil, it's even part of the economy and helps people pay their bills and live a better life. Here's another advantage: depending on the exchange rate of where you are in the world and the strength of the US dollar at the time, cheating out of the country is a great way to get wet for a really, really good discount.

Let's look at a couple of the best international destinations for getting your global cheat on in a safe way.

## Amsterdam

Amsterdam is one of the best places on the planet to cheat. First of all, the prices are reasonable: in most cases, it will cost you only about sixty to one hundred dollars to get your freak on. And it's legal.

You can walk the streets of Amsterdam alongside other tourists and locals and look at all the women who want to fuck you for money. The women are arrayed in windows like fine jewelry waiting to be purchased. How cool is that? It's a guy's form of window shopping.

And these women are not just the local women from that region; there are Spanish, Chinese, Caucasian, black, blonde, brunette, skinny, fat, hot, not, and whatever-the-hell-you're-into women. You can even watch a live sex show if you're into that. It's one of the last places on Earth where there is no stigma associated with sex. It's right there in the open next to a Michelin-starred restaurant.

What does putting sex out there in the open do?

It takes the dirtiness out of it. It makes it accepted and expected. It's the same sort of thing that makes it okay for a regular girl to whip out her tits at Mardi Gras in New Orleans. That same girl would never do that at a party in her hometown, but for some reason, it's not risqué when everyone is doing it. And in Amsterdam, everyone is having sex for money.

You don't have to walk down some dark alley like a creep, your head down so nobody sees who you are. You can walk right down the middle of the street with your head held high, knowing that everybody around you, for the most part, has the same creepy mission as you do.

In fact, there is a special area in Amsterdam where all of these sexual escapades are at your complete and public disposal. It's called the red-light district. Yes, there are red lights in the red-light district of Amsterdam, but they are used now more for ambiance than for their original purpose, which was to hide the prostitutes' red blemishes from venereal disease. Nowadays, you don't have to worry about your cock falling off, because the government regulates their snappers. How great is that?

As always, there are a few things you should know if you plan on traveling to Amsterdam for some snatch. First, the city actually has *two* red-light districts: the local district and the tourist district.

## The Local Red-Light District

The local red-light district is where most Amsterdammers go to partake in dirt, which is not to say that a tourist can't go there. You can. But there are a few things that make it different from the tourist district.

First, the local district is a lot smaller, consisting of only a couple of streets in a totally different part of town. It's the difference between going to Disneyland and Disney World. Are you going to have a good time at either place? Yes. But one has way more shit to do than the other.

Second, the girls working the local district are of lower

quality than the ones in the tourist district. Not to say they are awful-looking, but there is a noticeable difference between the two groups. The good thing about the local district is that it's less busy than the tourist one. So it might be a good place to start out, especially if it's your first time, before you head to the big leagues. You know, shake out your nerves and learn the ropes of how the whole procedure goes down, so that you don't look like an ass when you later find the girl of your dreams in the tourist district. It will also save you time and money.

## The Tourist Red-Light District

If you asked us what we thought heaven looks like, Amsterdam would be the first place to come to mind. When you are walking down its cobblestone streets with the majestic Dutch elms standing guard to protect the ancient canal and you're admiring the brothel windows, it is something to behold.

But you have to be careful not to get lost in all the historical beauty while you are trolling for the perfect sexual experience. It is as simple as walking around looking in a few windows by yourself or with a few buddies and finding a girl to bang. But there are still dangers and pitfalls to be found on the nostalgic streets of Amsterdam, so, as always, proper planning and procedure are important.

With any cheat, patience is always key, and this is especially true in Amsterdam. When you first hit the streets, your excitement level will be through the roof. You're going to feel the way Charlie did when he first entered the chocolate factory. But wait: slow down, walk around, and enjoy yourself.

Don't be Augustus Gloop and run right over to the Chocolate River and start drinking. You want to make sure you don't waste your money on one chick and then just two doors down find another girl who looks like the girl in high school you always wanted to bang, and now you're out of cash for the night. Or even worse, you've just busted your nut, and now you don't have any more gas in your tank to drive it home a second time. So take your time and make your first purchase a good one.

Once you've made your selection, you can negotiate a bit, but not much. Most girls have a set rate. If it's a slow night, the girl might be willing to let a couple of bucks slide here and there, but be prepared to spend the asking price. You don't want the girl you really wanna bang to tell you to beat it—and she will—over a few dollars.

A good rule of thumb is to ask what her rates are and then just walk away. That way, she knows you're interested, but you have a few minutes to think about how much you want that specific girl. And if your desire for that particular girl outweighs your stinginess, then go for it. It's as easy as knocking on her window.

After you make the deal, she will invite you into her room, which is usually right behind her. A typical room consists of a small bed, some dim lighting, and maybe a sink for freshening up. The girl will have the condoms and lube if needed. She will then ask you to pay. Don't be offended if she asks you to wash your junk in the sink before you get started; it's a good thing that she wants your dick clean. Also, don't be surprised if her attitude becomes more businesslike once she gets the money. Time is money in her business. She needs you to cum as quickly as possible so that she can make as many guys' fantasies come true in one night as possible. Remember, this isn't fine dining, it's fast food at its best. So don't take it personally if fifteen minutes into your humping, she breaks character because you haven't climaxed yet.

Just stay focused and bust your nut as soon as you can. When you're done, she will usually help you clean up and get you ready to head out the front door to do some more window shopping.

## Rio de Janeiro: The Motherland of Cheaters

The only other place that compares with Amsterdam is Rio. Imagine sitting at an outdoor café across from the surging blue waters of the Atlantic Ocean while sipping a fine dark roast Brazilian coffee and slowly smoking a cigarette, all the time surrounded by the most beautiful prostitutes on the planet—each of them waiting for you to give a head nod or a hand gesture to come sit with you for a spell and negotiate your fiendishly despicable plan.

Rio, unlike Amsterdam, can be a very dangerous place to score some tang. But we must say that for the true deviant, it's well worth the risk. The city has so many different ways for you to cheat, it deserves a whole book unto itself. Let's go over a few of Rio's dirty options for the cheater in you.

Much like other parts of the world outside of the United States, prostitution in Rio is an acceptable option for a girl— young or old—to make money. You just have to know where to go and what not to do while you're there.

## Termas

*Terma* is the Portuguese word for "spa" or "brothel." If you are looking for a great, safe place in Rio to cheat, we couldn't think of anywhere better. Think of it as a day spa for men, except that all the girls who work there are prostitutes.

We will walk you through visiting termas step by step so you know what the hell you are doing when you get there.

The first thing is to find a terma near your hotel, which is as easy as typing the word in the Search box on Google. They will give you an extensive list of all the termas in Rio, some with websites and price lists. They even have a Google map so you can map out the one closest to where you're staying.

Keep in mind that you don't want to venture too far away your first time out. Like we said, Rio is very dangerous. Its slums are some of the worst in the world, and if you don't have your head on right, you will get taken for all you're worth. So first things first: take a cab everywhere, especially at night. We don't care if it's two blocks away. You can easily hail a cab right in front of any hotel. Just tell the driver the name of the place you are going. It's not like this will be his first time taking a lonely American tourist to a terma.

When you make it to your destination, you'll see a couple of imposing bouncer-type guys at the front door. Don't be afraid; they are there for your protection as well as for that of the girls inside.

As you enter the building, you will come to a front desk reception area, where a lovely lady, or two, will greet you. She will ask you your first name only and explain the prices to you.

Once you agree that you would like to enter the establishment, you will be given a key attached to an elastic bracelet with a number on it. This number will be your identity and your method of payment while you're a patron. Everything goes on your number. You want a drink, show the waiter your number. You want some food, just hold up that bracelet and show them your number. And when it's time for some sex . . . you guessed it, it goes on your number too. That way, you don't have to carry around money or credit cards; everything goes on the number assigned to you.

Once you have your numbered bracelet, you will be directed to a locker room, where another fine lady will help you find the locker that corresponds to your number. This locker will be stocked with flip-flops and a robe for you to put on. At this point, you want to get undressed down to your birthday suit, put all your valuables in the locker, and lock it with the key attached to your bracelet.

Now you head up to the dance floor. There will be a room or multiple rooms with music playing and some of the hottest Brazilian girls you have ever seen dancing in nothing but G-string bathing suits, bikini tops, and high heels.

You might feel a little weird being in just a robe and flip-flops, but every other guy in the room will be dressed the same. Now you want to find a seat, order a drink, relax a little, and look around at what the place has to offer.

When you see a girl you like, all you have to do is wave at her, and she will come right over and sit down next to you. Some of the girls don't speak English very well, but this is a good thing. You don't have to worry about hearing about a girl's hopes and dreams of becoming a real-estate mogul. Instead you can exchange pleasantries for a minute and then, when you are ready, you can just say to her, "Let's go upstairs."

There is no negotiation because, from the minute you walk in the front door, everything has a set price, from the Coke you're drinking (three Brazilian *reals*) to your taking a girl up to her room. When you are ready to leave after your night of debauchery, they add up all the times your number was used to pay for things and present you with a bill. "Okay, sir, you had two sodas, one order of chicken nuggets, and three blow jobs. That will be three hundred fifty *reals,*" which is about two hundred seventeen fucking dollars. How great is that? Try that in Vegas—it'll cost you a thousand dollars, minus the chicken nuggets and two Cokes. You can get an even better deal depending on how strong the US dollar is, so it's a good thing to know the exchange rate before you go down there. You can pay cash or put it on a credit card. And don't worry, these people are professionals. The charge will come up as some restaurant chain in Rio, so you can just tell your wife that you took the boys out for a great dinner every goddamn night.

Visiting a *terma* is just one way you can get your cheat on in Rio. You can find girls while sitting at a café or dancing at a nightclub or buying some trainers at the mall. If a really hot girl comes up to you and seems interested, chances are that she is willing to fuck you for money.

But remember, unlike in the protective womb of the termas, everything is negotiable when you're out on the streets or in a club. So pick a price and stick to it. And don't forget that when you are talking money, you are talking *their* money. Don't agree to pay a girl "three hundred" for her services and give her three hundred US dollars. Be cheap when you deal with girls in the public sphere.

For one, you save some money. You also don't want them thinking you have money to throw away, because, as we said, Brazil is a very poor and dangerous country. If you're throwing around cash like it's nothing, a prostitute will probably tell her friends that you've got a lot of money, and you will find yourself held at gunpoint by a nine-year-old because his older sister told him you are rich.

Now, you might be wondering, "Okay, what if I meet a chick at a café, and she sits with me, and we talk and negotiate a price? Where do I take her then? Do I go back to her place? Do I find an alley?" The answer is simpler than you might think: you go back to your hotel room. All hotels in Rio understand that a lot of guys come there to cheat and have sex with the local women. So they are totally fine with you bringing a bunch of different girls up to your room while you stay there. And if you don't want to be seen walking into your hotel with a girl because you are embarrassed for some reason, you don't have to. In fact, as a general rule, it is probably best to tell any girl you hire off the street what hotel you are staying at, give her your name, and have her meet you there. This way, you can go ahead of her, get upstairs, wash up, and make sure that all your valuables are put away in the safe before she arrives.

These kinds of convenient amenities are going to cost you, but don't worry; it's not that much—maybe something like twenty US dollars. And it's well worth the price. What does that twenty bucks get you? Safety, that's what. A local prostitute has to check in with security at the front desk and give them her ID papers, which the concierge holds until she leaves. The only way she can get back those papers is to return to security and ask for them after she leaves your room. The front desk will then call you to make sure everything is okay. If you say that everything is fine, the girl gets back her papers; if you say, "No, the bitch took all my money and my Rolex," they will hold the papers and call the cops.

Hotel security in Rio is as tight as in some of our prisons in the States, but it's for your protection and safety. Don't ever, for any reason, go back to a girl's apartment or to wherever she lives. You will be setting yourself up for a horrendous situation.

For one, you don't have the hotel security to back you up if something goes down, and two, you don't know who will be waiting inside for you when you get there. Always take the girl back to the safety of your hotel.

To sum up the key points to remember while visiting Rio: keep a low profile, take a cab everywhere, know the place you are going to before you go, and whenever possible, have the girl come to you. If you do all that, you should have one of the most amazing times of your sexual life in Rio de Janeiro, otherwise known, to the truly deviant, as the motherland.

There are many other places we could cover when discussing cheating outside the country. There's Thailand, the Ukraine, and the Philippines, to name a few. But the rules are mostly the same no matter where you travel for your sexual escapades. Do your research and follow our rules, and you will have sexual memories you could never in a million years tell your grandchildren.

# TRUE CHEAT

**Account by Joe DeRosa, comedian, director, coauthor of this book**

**Outcome:** *fail*

The year was 2006, and I was dating this girl who I thought I was in love with.

Problem was, she wouldn't commit to me. Well, she sort of did. She would say, "I'm not your girlfriend, and you're not my boyfriend, but we're not allowed to sleep with other people." That really fucked my head up. I didn't know what it meant. Did she care about me but was too afraid to put a label on it? Was she playing mind games with me? Was she just confused? I didn't know. I did know, though, that I felt very strongly about her. I also felt very strongly about the fact that sometimes when I would call her, she wouldn't call me back for two days.

That kind of bugged me.

Anyway, a few months into the relationship, I got booked to do a gig in West Palm Beach, Florida, where the ass is as prevalent as the sunshine. My lady friend was on one of her "It's been forty-eight hours and I still haven't responded to your endearing phone call" kicks, and I was starting to feel really insecure and angry. So I'm sitting and stewing at the bar at the comedy club one night, waiting to go on, and in walks this beauty. As soon as she entered the room, I noticed her. And I was locked on her. I mean, I thought she was really, really, really, really hot. And wouldn't you know it, but what does she do? She walks directly to the bar, sits down next to me, and introduces herself.

Next thing you know, we're talking, she's laughing, and then it's time for me to go onstage. She watches me perform, and I have a crush-kill-destroy set. It goes off without a hitch, and I slaughter.

Now I'm really in.

After the show, we hit the town, drink it up, and have a ball.

Afterward, she drives me back to where I'm staying. My brain is screaming, "I know you're angry, bro, but don't do it! Walk away and go to bed!" But it's funny how a hand job from a hot chick in the passenger seat of her car can change your tune. So we go inside. We bang. And it's great.

The next night, I'm pacing around outside the club, thinking about the show I have to do and feeling extremely guilty. Suddenly, my phone rings. It's my lady. And maybe it was the goddamn Florida heat cooking my brain and screwing up my judgment or something, but, like a jackass, I tell her everything. *Everything.*

I honestly thought she might not care, since we seemed to have an undefined relationship. After I confess, she just says, "Okay. We'll talk about it when you get back. It's not the end of the world." Wow.

She loves me after all, right? Wrong. Apparently, what she meant by that was, "When you get home, meet me at a diner so I can tell you what a piece of shit you are and make you feel ten times worse while I cry in my chicken soup." And that's exactly what she did.

But she also picked up the check, so I guess it wasn't all that bad.

# The Fuckup

So young Joe DeRosa's a squealer, huh? Epic mistake. Never talk. *Ever.* Even if she's got you duct taped to a chair with a blowtorch to your balls and a pair of pliers locked onto one of your fingernails, never, never, ever, ever talk. She didn't even have to prod him! All she said was "Hello," and he blurted out, "I'm guilty! I did it!"

The biggest mistake Joe made was allowing his insecurity to fuel his motives. You can't do that. One of the most basic and crucial rules of cheating is that you need to act with authority and confidence. These things keep you focused and moving with poise. The second you get reactionary and use cheating as some sort of revenge tactic or ego pose, you're fucked. That's like robbing a bank because one of your friends called you chicken. The words "I'll show you!" should never be in your head when you're running around on your girl.

Truth be told, Joe may not have even cheated, technically speaking. It sounds like his girl's definition of a relationship was a little screwy, and that, understandably, got in his head and affected his behavior.

Was he really going out with her? Who knows? Even if he was, he probably shouldn't have been. All that "I'm your girl but not your girlfriend" horseshit is unfair. It puts a guy in an ambiguous position, leaving him unsure of how to act appropriately.

Still, for all intents and purposes, this story is a great example of what not to do when the pressure's on. Even if that pressure is all in your head and you misinterpret a simple phone call from your girl to be a heated interrogation.

DeRosa panicked. And not just in his confession. It was panic that led him to strange pussy in the first place. And it was panic that then caused him to immediately crack and come clean afterward.

That's two negatives in a row right there.

Never, under any circumstance, give in to panic.

Take a nod from Steve Buscemi's character Mr. Pink in *Reservoir Dogs*: "When things get tense, everybody panics. It's human nature. But ya panic on the inside. Ya panic in your head."

DeRosa panicked completely on the outside, like a shaking, shivering Shih Tzu.

The bottom line is that Joe just shouldn't have been cheating in this situation. He wasn't mentally prepared for the challenge and didn't understand where his quasi girlfriend stood in their relationship. You need to have a firm grasp on these types of matters before you step out. If you don't, shit goes wrong, as it did here. First off, DeRosa needed to be up front with the chick he was dating.

He should have told her, "I'm not going for this undefined nonsense. You're my girl or you're not." This would have cleared the air on a lot of his issues with her.

A statement like that makes the girl fly the coop or buckle down. Either way, it's a good thing. Who knows, maybe she would have reacted positively to his stern stance, and today they'd be married. Probably not. But we can dream, can't we? Joe didn't do this. Instead he trudged forward, allowing her to hold the reins and remain in full control. And because of this, he didn't know the facts. And because he didn't know the facts, he thought he had a free pass.

He didn't.

Although, he did get a free Reuben.

But still . . .

# Chapter 11

# The Greater Good
## Cheating to Save Yourself

Cheating isn't always a self-indulgent quest to get a taste of some new, untraveled trim. Sometimes it's something you have to do for your own well-being in order to better yourself or launch yourself out of a negative situation.

Let us paint a picture for you: you're in a long-term romantic relationship with a woman who is verbally abusive or, God forbid, physically abusive. She's the kind of gal who refers to you with a loving nickname like "asshole" or "faggot."

Maybe she likes to cause dramatic scenes in public. You know, the kind of shit where she gets drunk at a bar, and somehow, over the course of you trying to curtail her inebriated, obnoxious behavior, the bouncer ends up putting *you* in a headlock for not treating a lady with respect. Maybe she likes to hang on other guys at parties and flirt with anything that's got a dick and balls attached to it. Then when you accuse her of acting inappropriately, she snaps, "I don't know what you're talking about. You're being crazy!"

Meanwhile, if you turned your back on her in the men's department at Macy's, she'd probably dry hump one of the mannequins. Maybe she blames you for her lack of a career, yet every time she's offered a job, she turns it down because it's not the "right fit." Meanwhile, your bank account is hemorrhaging money like somebody just shanked it in the gut. Maybe she likes to throw shit at you during an argument. Maybe she cries every single goddamn time you disagree with her or criticize her.

Is there anything worse than a girl who cries all the time? Fuck.

Point is, if she does any or all of these things, the bitch is crazy. And *crazy* can mean a few things. She could be certifiable, where the only thing that will help her is eating pills out of a Dixie cup for lunch every day. She could have such low self-esteem that it's given her a persecution complex and made her think that everyone alive is secretly plotting against her, like she's Jason Bourne with tits or something. She could be so insanely childish that she doesn't give a shit about anybody but herself. Whatever it is, she's crazy, simple as that. But here's something that's not so simple: getting out of the relationship. You're in a tight spot, and you need to get out. But the longer you date a lunatic, the harder it is to bail. You keep telling yourself, "It has to get better. If it doesn't, I wasted all this time on the relationship." Well, it's never, ever, ever going to get better. You absolutely wasted your time.

Crazy women are just crazy, and there's nothing that you can do to change that. So stop beating yourself up and trying to figure it out. You made a mistake, which is okay.

So why can't you just leave?

Well, maybe you can. Good for you, if that's the case. But most guys are trapped for a variety of reasons. The biggest obstacle to bailing is your confidence. Usually, the woman you're with, even if she is walking hell, seems like the best possible option. Due to the wench's sick behavior, your emotions and morale have taken such a reaming that you can't possibly imagine being involved with someone more respectful, challenging, fair, or supportive than your current succubus. She's got her hooks in you bad. She's broken your spirit.

And there's nothing like the sight of an amputated spirit. There is no prosthetic for that. *Scent of a Woman*? Anyone? Nothing?

A lack of confidence also causes you to make decisions out of fear. You could be terrified to leave. After all, you're dealing with a wack-a-loon here. A confrontation with someone like that can be very intimidating. Chances are, you've already had several blowups with this girl over standard stuff. If any of those was even remotely scary, who the hell knows where she's willing to take it when some real shit goes down?

But again, that's mostly just your fear talking. You need to get your balls up to the point of realizing that it's all bark and no bite or that there are ways of handling a volatile situation.

Here's another potential snare frequently used by the unstable female: great pussy. A psychotic broad will usually have the capability of riding and waxing your bone with the enthusiasm and gusto of a highly trained professional. These chicks can be black-ops bangers. We're not talking standard porn-type sex here, we're talking the kind of screw that will stir loose juices and emotions buried so deep in you that they've almost fossilized. This type of thing will keep a gentleman hanging around longer than he should.

At the time, it will seem like a fair transaction.

"Mostly, she makes me feel like bird shit, but when it's fuck time, she makes me feel like all of the Avengers rolled into one." Well, guess what? The Avengers aren't real, and neither are those sentiments. Your diffident mind is tricking you into thinking your balls are worth more than your self-respect.

You need to find someone who will allow you to recognize how poisonous your current situation is:

Another woman.

And it may not be the first "other woman" you meet. This may take a few tries. What do you care if you're running around a bit? Fuck her, she's nuts! The point is, you need to jump back out there and learn firsthand that every female isn't hiding a pair of horns.

You may ask, "Why don't I just dump the woman I'm with and start over?"

Again, if you're able to do that, do it! That's the best-case scenario. But a lot of guys need to use their current relationship as a safety net while they shop the market.

Since you're already taken, when approaching new

women, you'll probably act with little to no desperation and be coming from a very genuine place. This is extremely effective when in pursuit of a score. Guys who are spoken for always do that.

Why do you think you suddenly have all these opportunities to bang once you settle down?

Once you've conquered some strange, it's quite likely that one of two things will happen: either the experience will grant you the self-confidence to split—after all, you're now desired by other women, and how could that not make your dick feel like tungsten steel?—or you'll actually meet the new love of your life and now have the urgent need to end the bad thing you're in and continue on with the good thing.

Look at it this way: you lost your mojo. And just like when Austin Powers lost his, you need to set forth on a mission to find it. That mission is new tail. Even if the sex isn't as insanely stimulating as what you're already getting, it doesn't matter. Remember, your most important interest here is your mental state, not your junk. Your goal is renewing your cool, not busting a nut in the most elaborate way possible. Therefore, in this particular case, don't go out and buy some ass.

That's pointless. You need to earn it. Earning is a powerful thing. It works wonders for a man's drive and ambition. Earning leads to owning. Earning is what built American industry. It's what caused man to discover new worlds: Space travel! The Internet! The Great Wall of China! Fonzie was an earner. James Bond was an earner. Every single Harrison Ford character ever was an earner. And earners don't take shit from anybody. So get out there and earn your mojo back.

You can do it. We believe in you.

# TRUE CHEAT

**Account by Colin Quinn, comedian, actor, writer**

**Outcome:** *fail*

Years ago, I was in LA. And the girls are like guys in LA; they'll cheat on a guy as fast as a guy will cheat on a girl. So I meet this girl. She was a dancer—as we like to say—and an "actress," and I really liked her. She asked me to go to some function with her, and we went and started talking about how we were both real "heart-breakers." I was about twenty-nine at the time and looked like Matthew McConaughey.

She was like, "Oh my God, we're perfect for each other be-cause neither one of us can hurt the other because neither of us has a heart." We discussed this on the first date.

Then we started hanging out, and she started dropping hints, saying things like, "Oh, I'm gonna end up getting into you and get-ting my heart broken."

Of course, me being a guy, I said, "Don't worry about it," while knowing that *could* easily happen. At the time, she didn't even know she was playing me. That's how good she was. She kept say-ing, "I know it's gonna happen. I'm gonna end up getting into you. I never get into guys. I break them, and I don't let them break me. But I can just tell . . ."

Meanwhile, I'm thinking to myself, "That is what's gonna hap-pen." But I said to myself, "You know what? This girl is crazy like me. I'm not gonna cheat on her."

I had just left the MTV show *Remote Control* and was on the road. So I'm down in Florida, which is where even the most monogamous people are allowed to cheat; it was Vegas before Vegas was Vegas. Everybody knew you cheated in Florida. I'm hanging out for a week, doing comedy, and all these girls are around me because they know me from MTV. I would go to bars, and it was absurd. I would judge wet T-shirt contests and have girls jumping all over me. Even still, I thought to myself, "You know what? I'm gonna be good."

I talked to the LA girl on the phone a couple of times while I was there. "Hey, what's up? Everything's cool." I should have noticed that she was being a little standoffish and a little bit weird, but I just figured, "She has intimacy issues. We both do."

My last night in Florida, I was hanging out with this girl who was wearing a red, white, and blue bikini and had won some sort of contest. She was one of the hottest girls I'd ever seen in my life. Even in Florida, people were like, "This girl's hot." Well, maybe a lot of it was her being tan, but she was hot. I had run into her three nights before that, and on this night, she just said, "Hey, come on, let's go back to your hotel." And I said to her, "I'm sorry, I can't. I have a girlfriend." And I'm sitting there thinking—even though at the time, it was painful; fuckin' painful—"You know what? Sometimes it's all about really being mature and making the sacrifice."

I come home the next day, get off the plane, and go right away to meet my girlfriend at a coffee shop. I say, "Guess what?" I'm about to tell her that I think this relationship really has a chance because I could've cheated in Florida, and she gives me a look like, "Don't say anything too nice." I knew something was wrong, but I figured it was something like she'd had a fight with her roommate. She had a look like, "There's a guy behind you with a fuckin' knife."

Finally, she said, "Before you say anything, I gotta tell you something. I slept with somebody last night."

I just went, "Oh. Oh. Oh." I turned, went to my car, and went home.

## The Fuckup

This tale weaves a strange morality. Colin didn't stray, didn't cheat, didn't get caught, but still, somehow, our pal fucked up. He fell for the old whore-with-a-heart-of-gold routine. We all do. Why is that? It's especially perplexing in this case, since Quinn himself was a whore. And over the course of this short-lived relationship, he actually did develop a heart of gold that allowed him to act with decency, character, and respect for the woman with whom he was involved. This sweet, sweet man, this cherub in human form, this majestic moral leader, managed to kindheartedly turn down an invitation into some tanned Florida snatch. And why? Because he so innocently assumed that the only pole his "dancer" girlfriend was spreading her legs for was the one at Club Cheetah.

Look, guys, the second a chick tells you she eats men alive, you need to cock your guns. And if you're the type of man who eats women alive, the second you start to have any sort of real feelings for a woman who claims to eat men alive, you need to cock your guns. Otherwise, bad shit is a-comin'.

Simply put: whenever you're thinking about not cheating because you're hoping that your lady will (hopefully) not cheat on you, cheat. Just fucking cheat. Goddamn it. Cheat.

# Chapter 12

# The Solitary Man

## Juggling Women While You're Single

Sometimes even the single man isn't really single. The average bachelor, if he has a hearty sexual appetite, can end up in a sticky situation without ever fully realizing that he did anything wrong.

You know how it goes: you're banging one chick (nothing serious, just a late-night kind of thing), when all of a sudden you meet someone else who you think might actually be relationship material. Before you know it, you're banging her too, but she's not your girlfriend yet. And given the fact that you're a man, you've probably got some other broad in a distant city whom you met on Facebook and have phone sex with once in a while—because it wouldn't be logical to fly her in for the weekend. Who the hell has money for that? We're in a recession.

Finally, on top of all this, there are the random gals you meet and take home from bars; the past booty calls that pop up occasionally; and all the other ladies you flirt with, planting sexual seeds for potential future encounters. It sounds like you're doing all right.

You've got enough ass to last five nuclear winters. But here's the problem: probably every one of those girls thinks she's the only one. Can you believe it? The nerve of these broads!

We know what you're thinking:

"I don't owe these girls anything. I never made any commitments."

That may be true. You might have even been candid (and ballsy) enough to tell every one of them that you're a walking hard-on that pops it in everything and, therefore, can't be tied down to one hole. Fine. But don't think for a second that these girls don't have their own angles. Although one or two of them may be cool with being a nightly drop slot, eventually one of the more respectable individuals is going to ask, "Where's this going?" So if you want to keep your sweet rotation of women going (which you should, since it's quite impressive!), you have to play by some of the rules that most spoken-for men are made to follow.

## Rule 1: Don't Be a Dick—to Yourself

There will be times during your juggling routine when you'll feel the slight pang of morality and ethics. You'll ask yourself, "What am I doing? Do I really want to live my life this way? Am I a piece of shit?"

Oh, you poor baby.

You're having too much sex with too many women. Boo hoo! Go cry to all the guys out there who can't actually fuck flesh and have to plug their joint into a pillow or some plastic. Go showcase your tears for all the world's prison inmates who have to bang a stinky, hairy bung while pretending that it's Kim Kardashian. Now, with that being said, yes, you are a piece of shit. But only by society's standards. Ignore these pangs. The only reason they occur is because something that was said on *The View* somehow affected your psyche. When you're eighty-five and death is approaching, you're never going to think, "I shouldn't have nailed all that sweet ass when I was a young stallion." Ride, stallion, ride.

Besides, you're actually doing yourself and your future monogamous mate a great service. Imagine: the average hump meets his sweetheart in high school, marries her immediately after college, and never has the pleasure of tasting another sweetheart's nectar. Then one day he wakes up at thirty and realizes he's going to go batshit if he doesn't get to pop someone else. *Boom!* Divorce. Picture your vast and diverse range of women as a trip to Baskin-Robbins, with your dick being that little plastic spoon. There are countless flavors to sample, and with that spoon, you can taste them all without ever having to commit to one. But when you finally do decide, you know that you're walking out of the ice-cream shop with exactly the flavor you want. This way, you'll never end up outside the shop screaming, "I knew I shouldn't-a got sherbet!"

## Rule 2: Shut Your Trap

When a man builds an empire like you have, it is a feat of such magnitude that it's only natural for him to want to bask in his own glory and share the news of his good fortune with others. Wasn't William Randolph Hearst in the public eye, taking credit for revolutionizing the newspaper industry? He was. And when you can afford to buy your own castle, you can be too. Until then, shut the fuck up. You don't want to be known as a male slut. If you look like Brad Pitt, that reputation is fine. But chances are, you don't. Most of us aren't 10s; we're 4s, 5s, and 6s, and, therefore, need to compensate for our physical detriments with personality, charm, and humor.

How personable, charming, and funny will you seem if everyone you talk to can't concentrate on what you're saying, since all they can think is "Why isn't this guy down at the clinic right now?" The bottom line is that any person you converse with is already going to think you're a pig.

Look at it this way: if you met a girl who'd banged everybody you knew, would you want to be seen with her in public? No. That street works both ways. Keep your dirty deeds to yourself. The only person who needs to know about them is you. Dude, you're Bruce Wayne, and Bruce Wayne doesn't talk about Batman to anybody—except Alfred the butler. So find your Alfred, and share your crazy nighttime escapades and adventures with him only. Then shut the fuck up and go back to being Bruce Wayne again.

## Rule 3: The Grand Pecking Order

Despite what God or any other inspirational figure has said, when it comes to the rotation, all women are *not* created equal. Some of them are winners, and some aren't. You may have a couple with whom you share some of your more intimate moments or have on your arm at your more important social events, but there are the others who are riddled with shitty personalities, bad hand-job skills, annoying character traits, and/or beer guts.

So you need to create a hierarchy.

The girl with the most "girlfriend" potential needs to be placed at the top. Even if she ends up not being *the one*, she's the closest thing to it, so she gets the prime seat. Then you order the rest of the stable accordingly. From best to worst, it's as simple as that. The best gets the most access to your life and your private affairs. The worst gets a horny, drunken phone call at four in the morning and maybe—just maybe—an Egg McMuffin for her troubles. You can't expose yourself fully and equally to every single cheat. There aren't enough hours in the day. You barely have time to tend to all the shit you need to do for yourself, let alone all the needs of all these women. Here's a list to reference:

**Top Cheat: Access Level 5.** This is your number one girl, so she gets most, but not all, of your info: cell and home numbers, permission to come to your apartment day and night, entry into actual "date" scenarios, and a slight knowledge of your background and interests.

**Second Cheat: Access Level 4.** A girl who looks as good as your number one but is slightly more annoying gets the cell number with limited apartment visitation: after seven o'clock at night only. She too gets to go on "dates," but only when your top cheat isn't available.

**Third Cheat: Access Level 3.** This is someone that you know you can't afford to get close to. Whether it's because she's too hot and will eventually crush you or because she's not quite hot or cool enough for a date, she rates limited access: your cell phone number and entry into your apartment after midnight only.

**Fourth Cheat: Access Level 2.** Despite her unsightly physical appearance or excruciating personality, this girl's uncanny ability in other arenas keeps her on the roster—but she gets the cell phone number, and that's about it. Whatever you do with her, do it at her place.

**Fifth Cheat: Access Level 1.** You met her on the Internet or while traveling, and the only thing she knows is your email address. She might eventually work her way up to the cell phone level, but for now, a dirty email here and there will have to suffice.

Now that you've established the hierarchy, you're able to effectively run your team. And by "run your team," we don't mean coach it. A pimp is a coach: someone who sends out his players to execute his strategy. You're a quarterback, right there in the game, getting your hands dirty with the other players, all working toward the same goal: to bang. Whether it's making a wide right or a buttonhook, your teammates need direction as to where to go so they can be wide open to catch the balls.

# Rule 4: Let the Garden Die

Following the previous step is not only for your protection and sanity, but also for your girls' benefit. It lets them all know where they stand without making them feel like pieces of garbage. If you play your cards right, it'll appear that you're depriving them only of time, not respect.

If they're not happy with how little you're delivering,

you're giving them an out. The less a lower-rung lady gets to know you, the less chance of her fully realizing what a hunk of shit you are and that she made a terrible mistake. By being neglected, she now has the option of saying, "Enough is enough. I can't do this anymore." Now *she's* made the decision to leave *you,* which is a good thing. Later on, if you ever see each other down the road, you're not the asshole who was fucking five broads behind her back, you're just the guy who was too busy to have a relationship at the time. She's going to appreciate that.

And who knows? Maybe she'll bang you again.

As these chicks find that you're not the man of their dreams and decide to split, let them go. Don't hold on. If you cling to one or two girls out of guilt or loneliness, you could wind up with the wrong broad. Sometimes the fifth cheat winds up as the last woman standing. And your dumb ass might, in a moment of weakness, become convinced that she's the one. She's not! A fifth cheat ain't never the marryin' type.

Don't get greedy, either. Greed leads to too much shit growing in your garden. When too much shit grows together, the roots from each flower become intertwined with all the other flowers, which means they'll be impossible to separate or rip out of the ground later. A good gardener plans ahead and systematically plants seeds along the way. That way, just as your roses are dying, the tulips are coming up beautifully.

But things aren't always so planned and perfect. You might get desperate because you look out at your garden one day and everything seems to be dead. Don't worry. Every good man goes through a drought. You have to trust that the rains will come, and your garden will bloom again.

# TRUE CHEAT

**Account by Gregg Hughes, aka Opie, radio personality,**
*The Opie and Anthony Show*
**Outcome:** *success*

I was doing local radio at the time when I met this girl, and we instantly fell head over heels for each other. It was a great, great relationship. One night her friend called me at the station to tell me that she was in a horrific car accident. A car clipped her, sending her twenty feet in the air, breaking both her legs badly, and leaving her with a possible head injury. Me, I'm thinking, "Okay, this is a slight detour. We're gonna continue with this relationship, and we can get through this." For the next four or five months, we "crutched" all over town and continued dating. I thought, "This is great! Things are gonna get back to the way they were before the car accident." Little did I know that would *not* be the case.

A few months later, I started to realize that this girl didn't like me as much as I liked her—and I was *really* into her. I decided that I had no choice but to move on. I was a young guy, so I started dating again, although I kept in touch with her now and then.

One day I get a knock at my apartment door, and it's my old girlfriend. I'm so excited. "Oh my God, this is great! I still have feelings for her, she still has feelings for me, she's here, life couldn't be better." Also, her leg had started to heal a little bit. She crutches her way into my bedroom and studies my bed. And she finds *one* black pubic hair. From somebody else. She loses her freakin' mind.

"How could you do this to me?"

I'm thinking, "Yeah, how could I do this to her?" But I'm also thinking, "Oh my God, I thought we were done!" Then I realize we *weren't* done; that she's still got feelings for me. She storms out, saying, "I never wanna see you again." I'm distraught, thinking I just blew this.

Fast-forward about a week. I come home one day, and there are about fifteen messages on my answering machine. I get excited, thinking I'm a very popular guy because I'm doing this radio show, and when I hit the playback button, it's her. She's on my machine with her ex-boyfriend. The entire time we were together, she swore that she didn't have feelings for him anymore. Well, *that* certainly wasn't the case, because message after message is of her and him having sex.

At one point she even said, "I'm getting eaten out. And it feels *really* good." And guess who the ex-boyfriend was? In the middle, she handed the phone to the guy "down below," and he taunted, "Hi, Gregg, it's_____." I knew him! I was crushed. If I didn't live on the second floor, I probably would have jumped out the window.

So now what do I do? I still had feelings for this girl, but you can't come back from that. She got me really bad because I had cheated first—or whatever. So I did the one thing any guy would do: I realized that I needed to get her back for *her* cheating.

Now, this girl's grandfather considered her an angel, and her mom thought she was the greatest daughter ever born. (She didn't have a father in the picture.) I decided to spend the afternoon playing all of the messages of her having sex with her ex-boyfriend on *their* answering machines.

## The Secret to His Success

This story will spin you in goddamn circles. It did us. We didn't know who was right or wrong or cheating or not or whatever—at least not until the end. At the tale's climax, it becomes painfully obvious that Opie had a vicious beast on his hands. Not only did she toy with his emotions by making him think that the relationship was over when it might not have been, and not only did she secretly still have some emotional and eventual physical involvement with her exboyfriend, *and* not only was that guy a friend of Opie's—Christ, we're losing track here. This chick was as crooked as the cops in the movie *Cop Land*.

Now, did Opie make a few mistakes? Sure. Well, actually, just one. We can't blame him for the pubic hair pinch. Who the hell would notice a lone pube? The fact that this broad could spot one means that she's wasting her time in whatever career she's pursuing; she should be hunting and sniping terrorists for the military. Also, Opie had no idea there was any reason to hide anything from her. She'd made it clear that whatever they'd had was over.

Here's where he screwed up: anytime you help nurse someone back to health and then put up with the trials and tribulations of hobbling all over town with them like they're Tiny Tim, you'd better expect some decent treatment in return. God bless us, every one! If, for some insane reason, you don't receive that courtesy, then the person you're dealing with is insane. We're not saying she had to pledge her heart to the guy for all eternity, but at least let the motherfucker down easy and don't mess with his emotions. But this witch beat on Opie until the bitter end. And why? Because he let her. That was his fumble. He should have counted his blessings the second she started freaking about that little, curly black hair. She was way out of line. But being love struck will distort your logic. Opie actually believed that *he'd* done something wrong.

At this point in the story, it seems like our pal is heading toward a nice, fat *fail*. Enter revenge. Sweet, sweet revenge. Holy shit! Opie went Charles Bronson in *Death Wish* on the chick. Playing the phone machine messages of her having sex with her ex for anybody would have been funny. Playing them for her friends would have been hurtful. But playing them for her family . . . wow. That's all we have to say. *Wow!* That's right, Opie. Don't take no shit from nobody. The score was more than evened.

# Chapter 13

# Getting Out Alive

*Call It Quits or Get Busted*

Every affair ends at some point, and it's best to do it on your own terms. You're in, now how do you get out alive? This is like dismantling a bomb. You don't want to cut the wrong wire, or else *bang*! And since every bomb is constructed differently, you need to know what makes yours tick before you try to stop the thing from exploding. Here are the methods we find most effective.

## The Fadeaway

This approach involves zero truth. It revolves completely around one thing: a magnificent, bald-faced lie that's vague enough to create distance, sympathy, and understanding.

Somebody died, somebody's about to die, you're about to die, etc. This thing needs to be *big*:

**The mark:** *Hey, are we still on for tonight?*
**You:** *I can't . . . my nana . . . I'm at the hospital with her . . . Oh God. I gotta go. I'm sorry.*

The goal is to make the mark feel sorrier for you than she does for herself over the fact that you're not available. You're not dumping her yet—or at least that's what she thinks. You're merely creating the illusion that you need some space.

**You:** *I gotta take some time alone. This Nana thing is crazy.*
**The mark:** *I understand.*

What she hears when you say this is "I have to back away, but not because of you." Psychologically, she needs to hear that it's not about her. When her ego doesn't get bruised, a crazy lady doesn't potentially chop off your penis. Only a real asshole would act selfishly in your time of personal crisis. So she'll give you her blessing. How beautiful is that? She's unknowingly supporting you as you slowly fade away. She has no idea that you plan to never see her again. The phone calls will continue for a bit. But eventually the calls turn into texts. Then the texts turn into emails. Then: nothing. You're gone.

The greatest thing about this method is the ambiguity of it. You never told the mark how sick your grandmother was or any details about the "tragedy" in your life. That means you can spin this story in any direction you want, so long as you continue to widen the gap. Here's another huge plus: when this is all over, you get to look like the victim. In case you end up running into the ditched woman or having to speak with her again, you can generate even more pity for yourself.

> **You:** *I'm so sorry things didn't work out between us. That stuff with my nana . . .*
>
> **The mark:** *It's okay. I'm sorry too. How is she?*

Your nana's fine, of course. Because nothing was ever wrong with her. You know who else is fine? You. And so is the mark. Everybody's unscathed. No harm, no foul. Thank you, magnificent, bald-faced lie.

## Just Disappear

This approach is quite simple, yet executing it can be trying, due to the high level of commitment needed. Disappearing means you do *exactly* that. You sever all ties to the mark, without any explanation or further contact. One day you were there, the next day you're not. Like a hacker that just got penetrated by the FBI, you cut the power, set the hard drives on fire, evacuate, and never look back. In doing this, you're chopping off the arm instead of painstakingly sawing through the bone.

Now, you'll almost certainly be opening yourself up to a lengthy stream of "What the fuck?" messages from your cheat. She's going to demand some closure. This is where you exercise your discipline. Be ice cold. Don't answer or respond to any calls, texts, or emails. That's it. And we're not oversimplifying this. That's all you have to do. You just don't exist anymore. And neither does she.

Wow. We're assholes.

## Mixing Lies and Truth

There's one more technique for a specific situation and a specific type of Romantic Cheater: mixing lies and truth. We explained it at the end of chapter 7. In case you forgot, go reread it. We're not typing it again.

## Getting Busted

Every great criminal runs the risk of getting busted. It's frightening, but part of the game. Whether you stupidly answer your cell phone while at a strip club, accidentally leave the porn video browser open on the computer, or have a psychotic mark show up on your doorstep, there are a million ways to get caught. Be aware of potential conviction.

The fear of this conviction is what makes a caper so goddamn exciting.

But you need to be prepared if the shit goes down. Strategy is as important here as it was during the planning stage. It doesn't have to be all bad.

Even though we have complete faith in the methods and philosophies we've given you, any decent handbook includes a section on troubleshooting. It's like when you buy a Blu-ray player: the little pamphlet tells you it's a great product, but it also lets you know what to do if the thing suddenly starts shitting smoke and catches fire. So here are some techniques for when you are confronted with your misdeeds:

### Ultimate Denial

Look no further than O. J. Simpson to understand how this approach works. No matter what evidence comes up during the trial, calmly and relentlessly claim that you are 100 percent not guilty. Never break. Your confidence and poise will work wonders in reassuring others of your innocence.

### The Indignant Argument Approach

When your girl has you cornered, you start an argument about ethics and privacy, accusing her of snooping around in your shit. The objective here is to get her to forget how angry she is at you and to start questioning her own behavior and morality. You'll also want to nurture her general feeling of guilt throughout the exchange.

### The Beautiful Mind/Shutter Island Technique

This is when you convince your girl that her assumptions of your infidelity are all in her head. You have to believe that too, like it's the truth. You've got to go into a Bernie Madoff mentality and literally get *offended* that she would think you did what you did. We know that sounds sick, but it works.

### Storm Out and Stay Away

Get so angry upon accusation that you scream your way right out of the house. And stay out. For a while. Let her worry about where you are and when you're coming home. Finally, she'll reach the point of not caring about whether you were faithful or not, she'll just want you back.

### The Camaraderie Routine

The mistress has confronted your wife or girlfriend with news of your affair. Tell your lady that the other woman is a psycho and that both of you may now be in mild danger.

Given the fact that safety is a person's first priority, your girl should agree to join forces with you against this outside threat. This will put her concentration on survival and not on your transgression. Hopefully, in the end, the two of you will have bonded and actually become closer as a result of your cheat.

## What to Do If You Catch Your Girl Cheating on *You*

Now that we've spent a couple hundred pages teaching you the fine art of becoming a complete piece of shit while simultaneously justifying your behavior, we would be remiss if we didn't add a dash of unwarranted indignation with just a hint of hypocrisy.

Women fuck around. And like the many layers of their vages, they have countless approaches when it comes to stepping outside of their relationship for an hour or two. The genius of women and their cheating is the prevalent belief that women rarely cheat. That their main concern is not physical pleasure. That they are more into financial security. In reality, women are just like men: most want to have their cake and eat it too.

There is an old saying: "A good man is hard to find." Well, a good woman is also hard to find. A woman that is 100 percent faithful is even harder to find. It's a harsh fact.

If your woman is cheating, and she's even remotely intelligent, you're never going to catch her. If the authors of this book were going to try to catch a woman cheating, we wouldn't even consider attempting to do it ourselves. We would hire a professional investigator and tell him, "Follow this bitch twenty-four-seven."

That's the only way you're going to catch a woman cheating, unless she is an idiot. With women, it's all about the misdirection. The makeup, the high heels, the push-up bras, the spray-on tans, the weaves, how they calculate the number of men slept with, and so on and so on—all of it is an illusion. You're basically dating Doug Henning with a pussy. Hiding any sort of side dick is child's play for them.

Another area that really helps women cheat is the male ego. A guy won't let himself even *consider* that his girl would ever step out on him. When a woman cheats on a man, a lot of people immediately assume that he didn't know how to please her in the bedroom. That public perception is so terrifying to most men, and can cause such emotional anguish, that the ego jumps in and calms the mental seas. It does so by refusing to allow the brain to even consider the gut feeling that the lady in question has been acting a little fishy lately.

So now that we've got our theory out on the table, what do you do if you catch your woman stepping out on you? It's simple: you have to dump her immediately, go through the pain of the breakup, and then move on with your life. A relationship is over the second the trust is gone.

We know what you're thinking: "Then what the fuck was the purpose of writing this book?!!!" *We don't know!* We're just like you. We want to be good guys, but we've got that demon between our legs giving us ideas with no exit strategies. So until someone learns how to wire a man to not fuck everything that moves, you need a book like this to help you navigate the rapidly changing technological waters of trying to fuck around occasionally.

## One Parting Word of Advice

If for any reason these techniques don't work, be a man and take the hit. You're caught. Deal with it. And always remember this last golden rule: Don't pull a Kobe. Never rat on your friends. That son of a bitch had his back to the wall because of his own actions, and in a desperate attempt to get the heat off himself, all he could say was, "Well, Shaq's doing it too!" What a pussy.

Sometimes you just have to man up. Go to a diner, order a sundae, and think about the life you used to have. You will find a new woman. And next time, when you cheat on her, do it without screwing up.

# TRUE CHEAT

**Account by Rich Vos, comedian**

**Outcome:** *success*

I was living with my girlfriend at the time, and I was in my fourth or fifth year of comedy. I was working this club, and after the show, I met this beautiful girl. I don't know why she came up to me; back then I looked horrific. I had long, curly hair and rotten teeth. I was horrible. Yet girls always used to approach me after shows. They don't now, but then again, I'm fifty-three and married with three kids. I say it onstage, so I guess I'm not the catch I used to be.

Anyway, this one girl came up to me out of nowhere, and I swear to God, the next thing you know, she's on her knees in the coatroom, blowing me. I'm thinking, "This is great!"

I can't believe how hot she is; just *so* hot. She *had* to be damaged. After the coatroom, we're fuckin' around in my car. She probably gave me a hand job or blew me again. I might've even had sex with her in the car, but all I know is that she had on a lot of perfume and makeup, so I smelled like a cosmetics counter at Bloomingdale's. I'm thinking, "I can't go home like this."

So I went to Red Tower, this hamburger joint in town that had chili dogs with the most powerful-smelling chili in the world. I got a chili dog, rolled down my window, and drove around holding the chili dog by my face and letting the wind blow the smell on me. Then I took some of the chili off the hot dog and wiped it on my neck and other parts of my body so that when I got home, my girlfriend said, "Oh, did you go to Red Tower?"

"Yeah."

"Why didn't you get me anything?"

"I didn't know you'd be awake."

## The Secret of His Success

What can we say? What you have here is a master at work.
First off, keeping his dirt in the comedy club was brilliant. No
cleanup, no neighbors, and no logistics to deal with. Just a
quick walk to the coatroom, and away we go. The only thing
you'd have to worry about is the coat lady coming in and
catching you. But fuck her. It's not like she's going to tell anybody. And even if she does, who's it going to be? The club
owner? He'd probably pat a guy on the back and give him a
bonus for having such a swell time after the show.

Now, Rich did eventually move things out to his vehicle, which is a bit more dangerous. Once you're outside,
you never know who may be walking by or if you might get
popped by the cops for indecency. That's a fucking nightmare. But given the skill level Vos displayed at every turn,
we have to assume that he knew what he was doing and
made sure the coast was clear for some literally auto-erotic
smuttiness.

The car does bring with it a few other potential pitfalls,
such as the left-behind scrunchie or the lingering stench of
perfume. But again, Vos is an aficionado and, therefore, a
man who flies in the face of adversity. The scents of Chanel
No. 5 and Maybelline enveloped Rich like a Snuggie.

This is where most guys would make their fatal error.

The average schmuck wouldn't even realize that he smelled like a Mary Kay rep. Then when his girl called him on it, he'd clumsily lie and say some stupid shit like "Some lady wearing too much perfume hugged me after the show." And the moron would keep repeating that lame excuse to the back of his lady's head as she walked out on him.

Other men would realize the presence of the incriminating scent and panic. They'd pray to God that the wind alone would bathe them of the proof of their infidelity or, worse yet, wash themselves in a public bathroom sink and come home reeking suspiciously of pink soap. Rich maneuvered beautifully around all of these easily made mistakes, allowing not knee-jerk reaction but innovation to steer his ship. A fucking chili dog?! Who thinks of that?! And he went as far as to rub the shit all over his neck?! What commitment to the cause. This brilliantly desperate action created a foolproof smoke screen.

Never in a million years would a woman encounter her man under these circumstances and conceivably think to herself, "He stinks of chili. He must have been fucking around."

Goddamn Jack Ryan couldn't concoct a conspiracy that would connect those dots.

Our hats are off to you, Mr. Vos. You truly are a game changer.

**SUCCESS!**

# CHEAT: THE MOVIE

The idea for this book came from a short film created by Bill, Joe, and Robert. The three wrote and starred in the comedy, which Bill and Robert produced and Joe directed. The story centers around a guy whose girl is out of town. He wants to cheat, but doesn't know how—so he goes to his friends, who are both masters of the art form, for advice.

Watch the film online at www.cheatamansguide.com.

# ACKNOWLEDGMENTS

Sincerest thanks to our managers at Apostle and 3 Arts, our agent, Lydia Wills, everyone at Simon & Schuster, and our friends who contributed to this book.

# I N D E X

# ABOUT THE AUTHORS

**Bill Burr**'s *Monday Morning Podcast* is one of the most downloaded comedy podcasts on iTunes, and he is a regular on Letterman, Conan O'Brien, and Jimmy Fallon. He will star in his third hour-long comedy special later this year.

**Joe DeRosa** is writing, directing, and starring in a number of web series, working on his third comedy album, and touring the country. He has been featured in his own half-hour Comedy Central special and two Comedy Central Records audio releases. He is a regular on *The Opie & Anthony Show* and Fox News' *Redeye*.

**Robert Kelly** is one of the top touring comics in the country. He hosts the popular *You Know What Dude?* podcast and has a recurring role on FX's *Louie*. His *Just the Tip* was an iTunes comedy album of the year, and his comedy specials include *Comics Anonymous, Comedy Central Presents Robert Kelly*, and *Tourgasm*.

**Follow @BillBurr, @JoeDeRosaComedy, and @RobertKelly on Twitter.**

Printed in the United States
By Bookmasters